The General Care Day Geckos

Sean McKeown

Table of Contents

Acknowledgments

This book would not have been possible without the dedication and unique cooperation among herpetoculturists throughout the world. This cooperation is virtually unparalleled in other fields of endeavor. It is with gratitude that I acknowledge those who have contributed in various ways.

I am especially grateful to Tim Tytle for his exchange of information on all aspects of the care and breeding of day geckos over a twenty-five year period and to Tom Digney for sharing his data on housing *Phelsuma* in enclosures in a greenhouse setting. Appreciation is also extended to Keith Lutz, Eddie Postma, Jurriaan Schulman, Willi Henkel, Dick Bartlett, Rick Hudson, John McLain, Dave Grow, Val Hornyak, Ron Gentzler, Doug Mader, Mary Morgan, J.M. Vinson, Larry Talent, Jayashree Ratnam, Jim Zaworski, Eric Nelson, and Barbara Bullock for sharing information on management, breeding, care, locality, habitat utilization, or other contributing data.

An illustrated publication is always enriched by the work of its contributing photographers. Deep appreciation is extended to Dennis Sheridan, Dick Bartlett, Ken Nemuras, John Tashjian, Jurriaan Schulman, Nick Garbutt, Sue Schafer, Breck Bartholomew, Eddy Postma and Rom Whitaker for their beautiful photography. Special recognition is given to Jane Bowden for her well executed area maps.

Thanks are extended to Tim Tytle, Philippe de Vosjoli, and Robert Sprackland for their review of the original manuscript and invaluable comments, and to Dorothy Delisle for her diligent initial editing.

The acknowledgments would not be complete without thanking the love of my life, my wife Wendy, who contributed to all aspects of this book and enriched it greatly. Any errors are mine alone.

Introduction

Day geckos have often been called "living jewels of the islands of the Indian Ocean," and with good reason. Many are bright green or blue with splashes of red, orange, and yellow. These brilliant colors allow for intraspecies recognition and help day geckos camouflage themselves among the brightly colored tropical plants and trees on which they make their homes. All day geckos are in the genus *Phelsuma*.

Gecko lizards are fascinating creatures in general. It may be hard to fathom in the 1990s, but almost all species of geckos were unavailable to the private hobbyist until the 1960s. One of the first books written about how to care for members of this diverse group of lizards was *Geckos as Pets* by Ray Pawley. Ray eventually became Curator of Reptiles at Chicago's world famous Brookfield Zoo. As a student at the time Ray's book came out, I was fascinated to see pictures of these unique animals in *Geckos as Pets* and in *Living Reptiles of the World* by Karl Schmidt and Robert Inger, and to wonder what they might really be like.

In the mid 1960s there was only a single major west coast reptile importer. His name was Ray Folsom and his establishment, Hermosa Reptile, was located in Hermosa Beach, California. Herpetoculturists came from far and wide to see the huge assortment of entirely wild-caught herpetofauna that arrived by the container load from every corner of the globe. This was a time when most wild places and wildlife populations were still truly wild and healthy, and reptiles could be encountered in the field in amazingly large numbers.

Once or twice a year, Ray Folsom would receive a small Madagascar shipment. With a little luck, it might include a few Madagascar giant day geckos and perhaps several of one or two of the smaller species of the genus *Phelsuma*. Color pictures of these lizards in books or magazines were virtually nonexistent. It was with a great sense of wonderment that I would look at these fast-moving, arboreal, bright green lizards patterned with splashes of reds, blues, and yellows.

Occasionally, I would purchase one of these animals and keep it in a terrarium with several live potted plants and an overhead light. Since suitable, commercially-raised insects were not available, wild-caught flies were the usual dietary fare. In the late 1960s a few day geckos would occasionally be imported into the United States and, by the early 1970s, a small but dedicated group of individuals began to work with them. During the mid 1970s importers began sending larger numbers of day geckos to Europe from the island of Mauritius and from the Comoros. Many of these were transshipped to dealers in the United States. Occasionally, in the late 1970s and early 1980s, small shipments would arrive from the Seychelles as well. In the early 1980s trade in captive-bred species began between specialists and hobbyists in Germany, Holland, other parts of western Europe, and individuals in the United States. At the same time reptile dealers and larger pet shops began to carry exotic species of lizards, including day geckos. Finally, in the mid 1980s, the island of Madagascar began exporting huge numbers of its lizards and other wildlife. Soon, a broad range of wild-caught Madagascar day geckos became available. A significant number of American and European captive-bred *Phelsuma* also entered the marketplace. At the time of this writing, virtually anyone who wants to buy a day gecko can get one, and at prices far below those of the previous two decades.

The purpose of this book is to provide an overview of lizards in this genus, emphasizing how they live in the wild, and the necessary information on how to properly manage and breed them in captivity.

From the beginning, I want to point out that day geckos can be hardy lizards, but their basic requirements must be met if these animals are to survive in captivity. In addition to the cost of the lizards, you will need to invest about $100 up front for a good terrarium, live plants, proper light fixtures, natural spectrum lighting, and a small sun spot light. You will also need a regular source for small, crawling and flying insects. If you don't have the funds or time, or are not detail oriented, do yourself and the lizards a favor and select some other, less demanding type of reptile, such as a captive-bred leopard gecko or corn snake.

In the last decade of the 20th century, wild places and wildlife are under seige by the huge, burgeoning human population. Everywhere habitat is being destroyed, and perhaps nowhere is this happening more rapidly or on a larger scale than on the large, 228,000 square mile (589,000 square kilometer) Indian Ocean island of Madagascar. It is our responsibility to manage lizard populations wisely and to strive to obtain day geckos that are either captive-bred, or at least field-cultured in the country of origin.

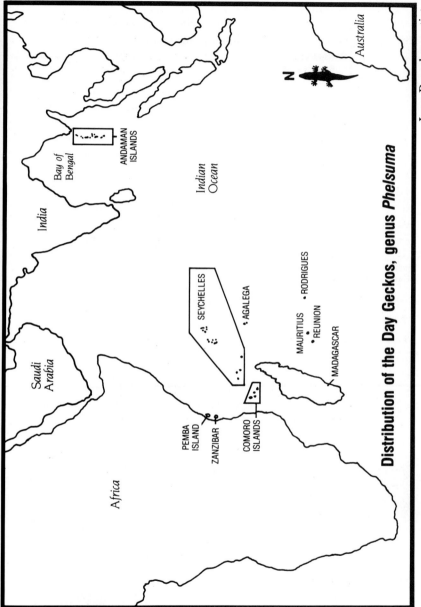

Distribution of the Day Geckos, genus *Phelsuma*

Jane Bowden, artist

ANDAMAN ISLANDS

Bay of Bengal

India

Indian Ocean

Saudi Arabia

Africa

Australia

N

SEYCHELLES

AGALEGA

MAURITIUS

RODRIGUES

REUNION

MADAGASCAR

PEMBA ISLAND

ZANZIBAR

COMORO ISLANDS

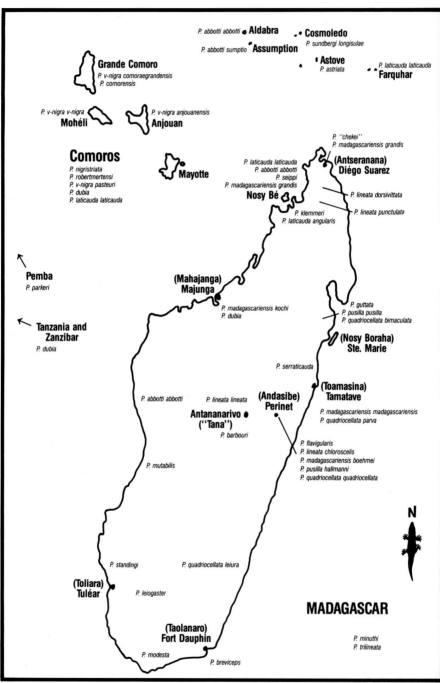

P. abbotti abbotti ● Aldabra
P. abbotti sumptio ● Assumption
● Cosmoledo
P. sundbergi longisulae
● Astove
P. astriata
P. laticauda laticauda
● Farquhar

Grande Comoro
P. v-nigra comoraegrandensis
P. comorensis

P. v-nigra v-nigra
Mohéli

P. v-nigra anjouanensis
Anjouan

Comoros
P. nigristriata
P. robertmertensi
P. v-nigra pasteuri
P. dubia
P. laticauda laticauda

Mayotte

P. "chekei"
P. madagascariensis grandis

**(Antseranana)
Diégo Suarez**

P. laticauda laticauda
P. abbotti abbotti
P. seippi
P. madagascariensis grandis
Nosy Bé

P. lineata dorsivittata

P. klemmeri
P. laticauda angularis

P. lineata punctulata

Pemba
P. parkeri

**(Mahajanga)
Majunga**

P. madagascariensis kochi
P. dubia

P. guttata
P. pusilla pusilla
P. quadriocellata bimaculata

**Tanzania and
Zanzibar**
P. dubia

**(Nosy Boraha)
Ste. Marie**

P. serraticauda

**(Toamasina)
Tamatave**

P. abbotti abbotti

P. lineata lineata

**(Andasibe)
Perinet**

**Antananarivo ●
("Tana")**

P. barbouri

P. madagascariensis madagascariensis
P. quadriocellata parva

P. flavigularis
P. lineata chloroscelis
P. madagascariensis boehmei
P. pusilla hallmanni
P. quadriocellata quadriocellata

P. mutabilis

P. standingi

P. quadriocellata leiura

N

**(Toliara)
Tuléar**

P. leiogaster

**(Taolanaro)
Fort Dauphin**

MADAGASCAR

P. minuthi
P. trilineata

P. modesta

P. breviceps

Jane Bowden, artis

- 5 -

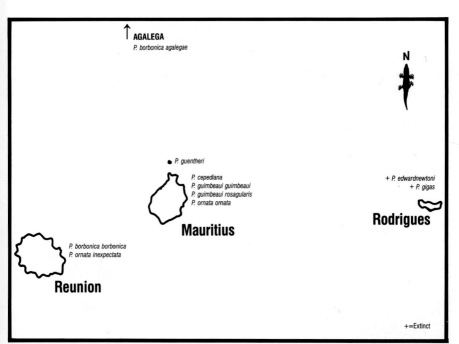

AGALEGA
P. borbonica agalegae

N

P. guentheri

P. cepediana
P. guimbeaui guimbeaui
P. guimbeaui rosagularis
P. ornata ornata

+ *P. edwardnewtoni*
+ *P. gigas*

Rodrigues

Mauritius

P. borbonica borbonica
P. ornata inexpectata

Reunion

+=Extinct

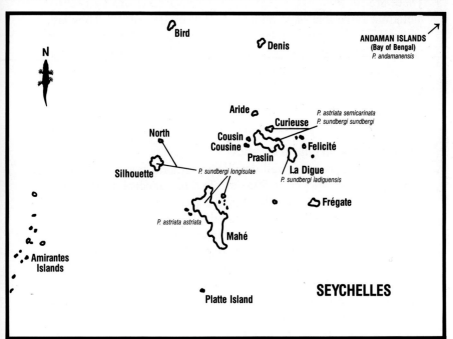

N

Bird

Denis

ANDAMAN ISLANDS
(Bay of Bengal)
P. andamanensis

Aride

P. astriata semicarinata
P. sundbergi sundbergi

Curieuse

North

Cousin
Cousine

Felicité

Praslin

Silhouette

P. sundbergi longisulae

La Digue
P. sundbergi ladiguensis

Frégate

P. astriata astriata

Mahé

**Amirantes
Islands**

Platte Island

SEYCHELLES

Jane Bowden, artist

General Information

All day gecko lizards belong to the genus *Phelsuma*, which is one of the many genera in the lizard family *Gekkonidae*. All members of the genus *Phelsuma* have a clear, fixed plate covering their eyes and lack eyelids. All day geckos also have toe pads, consisting of tiny lamellae, which can fit into irregularities on almost any surface. This makes it possible for the lizards to easily climb almost any vertical surface or plane. The thumb and inner toe are vestigial. Males have well developed femoral pores on the undersurface of the rear limbs. While most members of family *Gekkonidae* are active at night, members of the genus *Phelsuma* are active primarily during the day. Having evolved in splendid isolation on the subtropical and tropical islands of the Indian Ocean, their bright colors and vivid markings help them to recognize members of their species and to blend in with their colorful surroundings. Additionally, color pattern is an important differentiating characteristic as many of the taxa of *Phelsuma* exhibit only minor variations in the arrangement of their scales.

Distribution

There are 58 living taxa (species and subspecies) of day geckos, including some that have only recently been described. They are, with a single exception, endemic to Madagascar and the other islands of the Indian Ocean. One species inhabits the Andaman Islands in the Bay of Bengal (see area map).

Size

The smallest species of day geckos attain a length of only about 2.5 in. (6.5 cm) while the largest reach 12 in. (30.5 cm).

Secondary sexual characteristics

Male day geckos have well-developed femoral pores. Pores are absent or less developed in females. In a few species, including *P. sundbergi* from the Seychelles, females have rather large pores and are most easily sexed when the individual lizards are at peak coloration during basking. The femoral pores of the males take on a brownish-yellow or brownish-red tinge during basking and peak activity periods. Some day geckos, including the four taxa from Mauritius, are sexually dimorphic in both size and color or hue. Additionally, female day geckos may have well-developed endolymphatic chalk sacs on the sides of their neck for storing calcium, and in many species eggs may be visible through the ventral surface of the body shortly before the female is ready to lay.

Growth rate

How fast a newly hatched day gecko grows will depend primarily on how its environmental needs are met. Each species has certain daytime and nighttime temperature requirements and specialized feeding requirements. If properly maintained, smaller species of day geckos may be sexually mature within six to eight months. In larger taxa, the lizards may not be ready to breed until they are a year old.

Longevity

If properly kept and provided with the correct food items and vitamin-mineral supplements, it is not uncommon for small species of day geckos to live three to eight years. Under ideal conditions, individuals have been documented as living up to ten years. Larger taxa, such as the Madagascar giant day gecko, may live five to fifteen years with exceptional specimens living over 20 years in captivity.

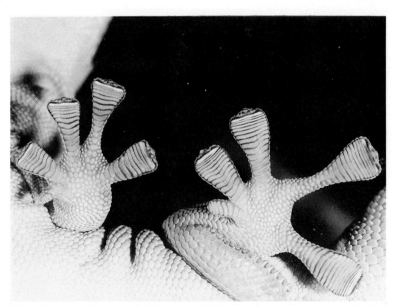

The undersurface of a day gecko's foot has multiple ridges for gripping tiny irregularities. This makes it possible for the lizard to run up and down vertical surfaces, and even to move quickly upside down across ceilings. **Photo by Dennis Sheridan.**

Commercial Housing of Day Geckos

Animal Importers

When possible, large shipments of day geckos sent to animal dealers from Madagascar or other countries of origin initially should be unloaded into large, vertical enclosures. The lizards will need to be misted regularly and offered several large, shallow plates of peach or apricot baby food, as well as appropriate size crickets. High mortality may occur if the lizards do not have multiple climbing areas and suitable basking areas. If outside temperatures are in the 70-85°F (21-29° C) range, large screened enclosures can be wheeled outside. Natural sunlight and good airflow will do much to alleviate the stress the lizards are subjected to in capture and transit.

Many reptile importers and wholesalers may not have the facilities to provide large screened enclosures and will need to house numerous day geckos in a way that conserves space and time. The following methods will help to maintain the good health of the lizards in a temporary situation if, due to space and labor considerations, they cannot be managed as outlined above.

A Madagascar giant day gecko peacefully surveys his domain in a well-planted vivarium. Photo by Dennis Sheridan.

1) When a large shipment of day geckos comes in, the first step during the unpacking process should be to remove and segregate any sick, thin, or injured lizards from the main group. This will reduce the risk of disease being spread and will allow sick, stressed, or injured animals the opportunity to recover. In large groups, the healthier animals will compete more effectively for space and food than weakened or unhealthy individuals.

2) Day geckos should be housed in groups by species. It is desirable, when housing these lizards temporarily in groups, not to provide so much space that the animals can establish territories. For example, a standard 30-36 in. (76-91 cm) screened top vivarium can temporarily house approximately 50 of the smaller day geckos, such as the commonly imported wild-caught species, such as *Phelsuma dubia, P. guttata, P. laticauda* and *P. lineata.*

A 48 in. (122 cm) vivarium can temporarily house 30 larger day geckos, such as *P. madagascariensis.* To date, no study has been done to determine optimal management procedures for large groups of day geckos. Until the factors associated with territoriality and intraspecies aggression in high-density groups have been isolated, these procedures should prove useful. When maintaining these animals in large groups, monitor at least twice daily to remove unusually aggressive specimens and/or weakened or stressed animals.

3) Substrate. With groups, quick- and easy-to-replace substrates are recommended. Newspaper, orchid bark and artificial grass mats have been used successfully.

4) Enclosures containing large numbers of day geckos should be appropriately landscaped with essential cage structures, such as vertical shelters and resting areas that are horizontal or at a slight angle. Simple vertical shelters can be constructed by nailing three boards together in an H pattern. In tall enclosures, it may be necessary to add a base to these shelters for stability.

Horizontal structures can be readily built by using 2x4 in. (5x10 cm) sections of wood. These structures can be easily disinfected between shipments by using a 5% bleach solution and then rinsing thoroughly.

5) Temperature. The temperature in the enclosures should be maintained at 80-87°F (27-31°C). This is best done by keeping the vivaria in a heated room. Most reptile dealers maintain their facilities at this temperature range, so this should not be a problem. If there is

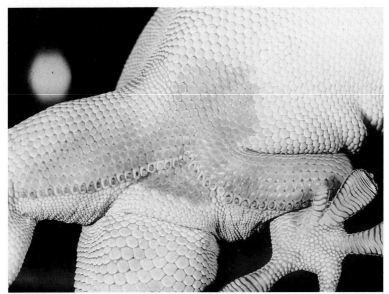

The only accurate way to sex a day gecko is to visually observe the area surrounding the vent. As shown here, males have enlarged femoral pores; also, slight hemipenile bulges just past the vent at the base of the tail. Photo by Dennis Sheridan.

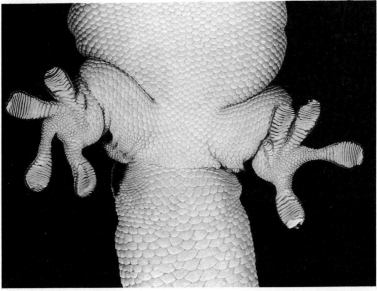

The underside of a female day gecko. Note the absence of enlarged femoral pores. Photo by Dennis Sheridan.

a problem, then spotlights, incandescent lights and, if all glass vivaria are used, subtank heating systems such as Flex-Watt® can be used.

6) Lighting. For short-term housing, day geckos will fare well using either incandescent or plain fluorescent lighting over their enclosures. Avoiding high intensity lighting may reduce the probability of aggression when maintaining day geckos in large groups on a short-term basis.

7) Food and water. All newly imported day geckos are invariably dehydrated. They should be offered water through misting at least twice a day.

A commercial nectar used to feed lories and lorikeets (nectar-feeding parrots), supplemented with calcium/vitamin D3 mix, will provide quick and inexpensive nutrients to these geckos. The mix should be prepared as indicated and offered in shallow containers. Watch for ants, which will be attracted to this food. Easily obtained alternatives are banana and peach baby foods. Calcium and vitamin D3 supplements can easily be added to these foods. In addition, commercially raised crickets of an appropriate size should be offered at least every other day. Small day geckos require one to two week old crickets. Medium size taxa will feed on two to three week old crickets and wax worms. Larger day geckos should be given four to five week old crickets and wax worms. The crickets should be coated with a powdered calcium/vitamin D3 supplement at each feeding.

Note: The above instructions will allow for the short-term maintenance of large groups. As groups become smaller, aggression and territorial behaviors will be noticed and additional segregation will be required. With rare species, imported in small numbers, individuals should be maintained singly or in sexual pairs. Females of delicate small species, such as *P. cepediana,* will generally not fare well if maintained in groups, and should be housed individually to minimize mortality.

Pet Shop Care

Number of animals per enclosure

Once the lizards have been sent to the pet stores, it is necessary to house them within a room or section of the store which provides temperatures in the 80s°F (27-32°C) during the day and 70s°F (21-26° C) at night. On a temporary basis, small- and medium-size day geckos should be housed singly in 5 gallon (19 liter) vivaria or in pairs in 10 gallon (38 liter) vivaria. Large species can be housed singly in 10 gallon (38 liters) vivaria. Using larger size vivaria and additional live plants, a sexual pair or two females of a large size species may be housed together. Generally, it is not a good idea to mix species, especially taxa of different sizes, since this may lead to extreme stress and/or the larger eating the smaller.

Substrate, cage furniture, and lighting

Topsoil is an excellent substrate. Artificial turf (Astroturf®) may also be used on the enclosure floor, but crucial humidity levels may be too low. To correct this and cut down on stress, include live potted plants in the enclosure. Small- and mid-size species of day geckos require one or more house plants, each in a 1/2 gallon (2 liter) plastic container with potting soil. If Styrolite® (tiny pieces of white styrofoam) is in the potting soil around the plants, cover the Styrolite® with an additional inch of Styrolite®-free potting soil or clean topsoil. This is necessary because the lizards may accidentally ingest pieces of the styrofoam while feeding. For large species of day geckos, one or more gallon-size potted plants will be necessary per enclosure. Snake plant *(Sansevieria)* is the preferred species of plant for large day geckos housed in a temporary holding situation. Water the plants intermittently so that the soil dries out between waterings. In order to keep the humidity high enough in the enclosure, heavily mist the plants twice daily. It is helpful if the sides of the vivaria are not transparent so that the day geckos are not stressed by close visual contact of other lizards or reptiles. Commercial natural backgrounds are available. As an alternative, colored paper (light colors such as green, blue, yellow, or white are preferred) can be affixed to the outsides of the back and sides of the enclosure. The vivaria should be placed under full-spectrum lighting, such as Vitalite® and/or BL blacklight. Plants in each enclosure will provide suitable areas for climbing. The top of the enclosure should allow for good air flow so that the air inside is not stagnant.

Watering and feeding requirements

A portion of each enclosure should be misted with lukewarm water from a spray bottle once in the morning and once in the late afternoon. It is best for day geckos to drink from water sprayed on the sides of the enclosure and plant leaves rather than using a water dish, as this is similar to drinking rain water in the tropical areas from which they come. It is often useful to add several drops of liquid multivitamins to the water which is to be misted. (Avitron® or ABDEC® will work fine.) A baby food jar lid with banana or peach baby food or a small amount of mixed Nekton Tonic® or a lory nectar should be placed on the bottom of the enclosure. The lizards should be offered insect food every other day. Generally, a lizard will eat three or four insects at a feeding. For small- or mid-size species of day geckos, offer first stage (one week old) crickets, or small wax moth larvae. For larger forms, offer sub-adult crickets and wax moth larvae. It is important not to allow a build-up of uneaten insects for two reasons. First, any such insects will have lost their vitamin/mineral coating. Secondly, un-eaten insects will continue to grow and may reach a size where they are capable of inflicting injury on the lizards themselves.

How to construct an outdoor enclosure for day geckos. Such enclosures are suitable when the daytime temperatures are 75-95°F (24-35°C), and the nighttime temperatures do not drop below 60°F (16°C). The planting must allow for both sun and shade. Photo by the author.

Information and products the customer will and will not need

In order that the customer may properly care for the lizards that he/she purchases, label each enclosure with both the common name and the scientific name of the lizard within. The customer may need to look up information on that species using the scientific name. Additionally, an aluminum reflector with a 60 watt bulb or low wattage spotlight will be needed. It should be placed over one end of the enclosure to provide a warm place under which the lizards can bask. Note: *Hot rocks and heating pads are NOT suitable heat sources for these arboreal lizards. Be sure to convey this information to the customer.*

Generally, the best commercially made enclosures for day geckos are those that have a sliding inset screen top with a set pin, such as those made by Sta-In Reptile®. These vivaria may be 10 gallon (38 liter) or larger, regular, high, or hexagonal-shaped tanks. The key is an inset sliding screen top with a set pin. As a rule, the more vertical the format and the larger the vivarium, the better the lizards will fare. Additional potted plants will need to be purchased to provide a suitable environment.

In addition to the lizard or lizards and the appropriate enclosure, the customer will also need to purchase vitamin/mineral supplements for dusting the food items presented. These should include calcium carbonate and vitamin/mineral supplements made specially for lizards. Several suitable products that meet these needs are shown below. Instructions are also given for dusting food items with these products.

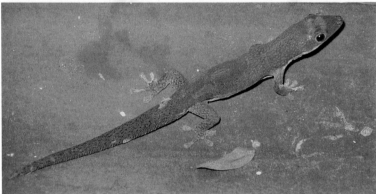

Phelsuma antanosy, a newly described species of day gecko from southeast Madagascar. Photo by C.J. Raxworthy.

Mid-size indoor day gecko breeding enclosure designed by the author at Chaffee Zoological Gardens of Fresno, California. Door and screening have not yet been added. Page 127 photo shows details of the interior of this enclosure. Photo by the author.

Managing Day Geckos as a Hobbyist or Breeder

Selecting an enclosure

Select as large, as high, and as nice an enclosure as you can afford. One of the nice things about keeping day gecko lizards is that you can create a beautiful vivarium setting that could look like a small section of some gorgeous tropical landscape on a beautiful island that you might wish to visit on vacation. This is the way day geckos are managed in Europe and with great success.

Ground medium

Good quality topsoil or Styrolite®-free potting soil makes an excellent ground media. It is not good to use sand or small gravel because it might accidentally be ingested and could cause intestinal blockage problems or even death. Fine or seedling grade orchid bark has also been used successfully by commercial breeders. Live plants are simply placed in their pots in the orchid bark or topsoil.

Note horizontal basking strips at the top of the vivarium to allow for basking under full-spectrum lighting. Photo by Dennis Sheridan.

Landscaping the vivarium

Place a 0.5-1 in. (1.3-2.5 cm) layer of pebbles at the bottom for drainage, followed by a 1.5 in. (3.8 cm) layer of sandy potting mix (peat-based potting soil with 1/3 sand) and a top layer of several inches of good quality topsoil. Live plants, such as snake plant *(Sansevieria),* bromeliad, orchid, split-leaf philodendron *(Monstera), Dracaena, Pothos,* Chinese evergreen *(Aglaenoma),* and other tropical plants available at your local nursery, in 1/2 gallon (2 liter) or 1 gallon (4 liter) containers, may be planted directly in the ground medium or transplanted into small pots which should be buried so that only the top of the pot is exposed. Next, cut sections of bamboo stalks and sink them into the ground to provide both sturdy vertical and semi-horizontal climbing areas for the lizards. For large species of day geckos, you will need to use sections of giant bamboo in which the females can lay their eggs. Bamboo sources can be found in yellow-page phone directories and at some import stores. It may take some investigation to find a source. Some additional information on this is provided in the species accounts.

A female Standing's day gecko licks water off her face just after being misted. Photo by Dennis Sheridan.

Lighting

Adequate lighting should be provided in any vivarium containing day geckos and live plants. You will need two or more full-spectrum fluorescent tubes, such as VitaLite® or BL blacklights, running the length of the top of the enclosure. The former are available through Duro-Test Corp.; the latter can be obtained at large hardware stores. If you use blacklights, be sure to use BL blacklights and not BLB blacklights, which are designed for posters rather than lizards. These fluorescent tubes can be 2 or 4 ft long (61 or 122 cm). They fit into shop light fixtures available at your local hardware store and are rather inexpensive. The full-spectrum lights are somewhat more costly.

Heating for display enclosure

Because day geckos come from tropical and subtropical areas, they need daytime enclosure temperatures of 82-88°F (28-31°C) and nighttime enclosure temperatures of 68-75°F (20-24°C). In a planted vivarium, incandescent bulbs can be used over specific basking areas to provide additional heat for basking, as well as basic background enclosure heat. Do not use hot rocks and heating pads; these are useless for small, arboreal lizards. A thermometer may be used to monitor the temperature of the basking area as well as the ambient air in other parts of the vivarium. To get a correct reading, the thermometer must be placed at the bottom of the tank at different specific locations. The purpose of the thermometer is to determine temperatures in the enclosure; it does not remain in the vivarium. If room temperatures in your house vary on a seasonal basis, readings should be taken in each enclosure every few months. Room temperatures will probably influence those of your enclosures. At night, low wattage red incandescent light bulbs can be used for heating, if necessary.

Relative air humidity

Most day geckos need a relative air humidity of 50-85%. Refer to the species accounts as to which taxa come from areas that have high humidity and rainfall. Humidity can be increased by watering portions of the ground substrate on a daily basis. At the same time, the enclosure should dry out by the end of the day. You do not want to create a constant, overly moist environment. Excessive moisture can lead to infections of the skin and toe pads. If you live in a very dry climate, a room humidifier may be used to increase the humidity level for your entire day gecko room.

Misting the plants twice a day will also help increase relative humidity. Day gecko managers who wish to keep the enclosure glass spotless are well advised to use purified water as tap water often contains dissolved minerals which, over time, stain the glass sides of the vivarium.

Vivarium maintenance

A regular maintenance schedule is necessary to maintain an attractive environment and provide a healthy place for the lizards to live. Remove fecal matter from the glass sides of the vivarium, on a routine basis, using a moist paper towel. Feces on the ground can be removed with the aid of a long-handled plastic or metal scoop which you can purchase at your local hardware or garden store. This aspect of maintenance needs to be performed once or twice weekly. Besides detracting from the beauty of an enclosure, allowing a build-up of fecal matter can present a serious health problem to the lizards by promoting a potential build-up of internal parasites or other pathogens. The entire vivarium substrate should be replaced every three months as part of this preventive health strategy.

Vertical-format vivaria housing day geckos in a greenhouse setting. Photographed at Tom Digney's breeding facility by Ken T. Nemuras.

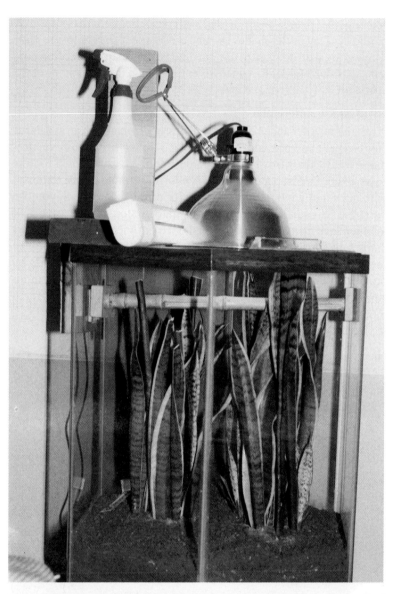

This vertical vivarium, designed for keeping a pair of adult *P. standingi*, is an example of a minimum enclosure design for proper maintenance of day geckos. This would also be suitable for most species of day geckos. Note soil substrate, screen top, bamboo perches for basking, snake plants, full-spectrum fluorescent lighting and sun spot in an aluminum reflector. All day geckos will need to be misted once or twice daily to provide water. Photo by Dennis Sheridan.

The day gecko as a pet

A day gecko should not be thought of as a lizard "pet" in the sense of an animal to handle and interact with frequently. *Phelsuma* are best thought of as display lizards. Only a few taxa, such as the Madagascar giant day gecko *(Phelsuma madagascariensis grandis)*, Koch's day gecko *(Phelsuma madagascariensis kochi)*, Standing's day gecko *(Phelsuma standingi)*, and the Seychelles giant day gecko *(Phelsuma s. sundbergi)* will typically tolerate any handling. These species, although they may come over and take an insect from a pair of forceps or from between your thumb and forefinger, should not be grabbed, as their delicate skin can be easily damaged or ripped. Occasionally, adults of these large, less stress-prone species may be taught to rest on a hand or shoulder for a short time. However, this should not be tried with hatchlings or juveniles as it may prove stressful.

If you are looking for a pet lizard that readily tolerates frequent handling, your best choices are Australian blue-tongued skinks *(Tiliqua scincoides intermedia, Tiliqua s. scincoides)*, Australian bearded dragons *(Pogona vitticeps* or *Pogona barbata)* and captive-raised green iguanas *(Iguana iguana)*.

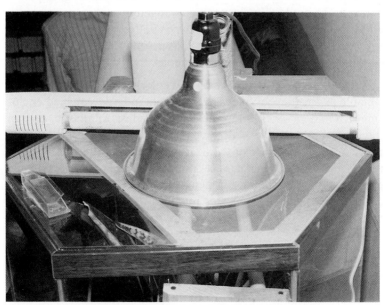

Lid of a day gecko vivarium. Note screen top to allow air flow, full-spectrum lighting and 75 watt sun spot light in aluminum reflector. Photo by Dennis Sheridan.

Vivarium Setups for Day Geckos

Indoors

Vivarium I is a planted vivarium with good airflow. It should have an earth bottom, live plants, and hollow stems or pieces of cork bark for hiding. It is best suited for geckos that are arboreal, but which do not come from either an extremely dry climate or from a rainforest.

Vivarium II is a rainforest vivarium with thick planting. Use topsoil or humus substrate. European breeders like to cover the sides and back with corkbark. Use many live plants and vertical bamboo sticks so that the lizards do not feel stressed. This enclosure can include bromeliads and orchids and be made quite attractive to the human eye.

Outdoors or in greenhouses

The serious day gecko breeder should have suitable outdoor **screened** enclosures for day geckos when the temperature is between 70-89°F (21-32°C). The lizards must be taken in if the temperature gets significantly hotter or cooler. Outdoor enclosures should be relatively large and should have good airflow. The enclosure should afford part sun and part shade. It is critical that the plantings or potted plants in the outdoor enclosure are arranged in such a manner as to allow the lizards to move easily between both sun and shade. A drip system over a portion of the enclosure may also prove useful, especially during hot summer afternoons.

Most day geckos only show their best coloring when the weather is suitable and if they are managed outdoors in large screened enclosures. Outdoor enclosures must not be glass or plastic, as sun traveling through either will increase temperatures drastically, rapidly causing the demise of the lizards. The enclosure must also be reasonably sturdy so that it is cat-, dog-, rat-, and bird-proof. Outside enclosures must be roomy and include a number of suitable plants for climbing. Check thermometer readings in the late morning and afternoon to be certain the temperature parameters are correct.

Vivarium I. This vivarium is designed for geckos which are arboreal but not from rainforest areas. A well-drained potting soil (30% pumice or crushed porous rock) is used as a substrate. *Sansevierias* and small *Dracaenas* grow very well in this type of setup. Bamboo stems or pieces of cork bark should be provided for hiding. Note the two types of lighting recommended for keeping day geckos. Drawing by Glen Warren.

Vivarium II. This vivarium, recommended for day geckos requiring higher relative humidity, has a substrate of potting soil over a drainage layer. Bromeliads, pothos, *Dracaenas* and Chinese evergreen will work well in this environment. Hollow bamboo stems can serve as basking areas as well as shelters. If cork is used as a background, epiphytic plants can be grown in this type of vivarium. Drawing by Glen Warren.

Feeding

In the wild, day geckos feed on insects, other invertebrates, nectar, and pollen. This book will outline how to provide a similar diet for these lizards in captivity.

Size of prey for feeding day geckos

Generally, day geckos can be categorized in three sizes: small, 2 1/2-5 in. (6.4 - 12.7 cm) in total length; medium, 5-8 in. (12.7-20.3 cm); and large, 8-12 in. (20.3-30.5 cm). Small species should be fed hatchling (pinhead) or one week old (first stage) crickets, wingless fruit flies, and flies. Medium species may be fed two and three week old (second and third stage) crickets, wax moths (adults and larvae), and flies. Large species may be fed four and five week old (fifth stage) crickets, wax moths (larvae and adults), flies, mealworms, up to half-grown superworms, and butterworms (Chilean caterpillars).

Crickets *(Acheta domestica)*

Crickets are available in six different stages or sizes ranging from pinheads to large-winged adults. When ordering, refer to the following sizes: hatchling, one week old, two weeks old, three weeks old, four

Common house crickets *(Acheta domestica)* are an ideal source of food for most day geckos. They should be dusted with a vitamin/mineral supplement and offered at a size that is appropriate for the species being kept. Photo by Dennis Sheridan.

Adult female crickets will lay their eggs in a dish of slightly moistened vermiculite at the bottom of the cricket enclosure. If kept warm, the eggs will take about three weeks to hatch into "pinhead" size first stage crickets. Photo by Dennis Sheridan.

Pinhead size hatchling crickets are an ideal food source for neonates and juveniles of smaller species of day geckos. Photo by Dennis Sheridan.

weeks old, five weeks old, and adult. Crickets can easily be obtained directly from commercial cricket farms, reptile wholesalers, or large pet shops specializing in reptiles and/or amphibians. Crickets are an important staple in the captive day gecko diet. They can be obtained year round in a variety of suitable sizes. Correctly sized, their exoskeleton is not a problem and their chitin content is relatively low. Additionally, the crickets can be nutritionally power fed alfalfa leaves, oats, Layena® chicken egg-laying mash, and cricket mash.

Wax moths *(Gallera melonella)*

These are typically shipped in the larval or caterpillar stage, usually from breeders in the midwest. These insects can be purchased directly from the supplier through the U.S. mail, or bought in a plastic container from a local fish bait store or large reptile-oriented pet shop. When these larvae, known as wax worms, are shipped by the breeder, they are removed from the honeycomb they normally live in and are packed in wood shavings. Shavings are thought to protect the caterpillars against excessive heat or cold. The problem is that wood shavings may accidentally be ingested by lizards and can result in intestinal obstruction and even death. Therefore, the larvae need to

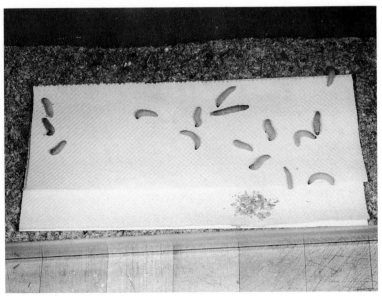

Wax moth larvae *(Galleria)* can be used as one component of a varied day gecko diet. Crickets should be offered at alternate feedings. Most day geckos should be fed on an every other day basis. Photo by Dennis Sheridan.

be individually transferred into a clean container of bran meal to which a slice of honeycomb has been added. Honeycomb can be obtained from beekeepers, markets, or health food stores. The wax moth larvae can be housed in this way until ready to be fed out. However, be aware that wax worms, despite their soft exoskeletons, are hard to digest. They have a high fat content and are not as nutritionally balanced as crickets. Therefore, wax moth larvae should be offered to day geckos more as a supplement than as a primary food source. Care should also be taken to feed smaller, partially grown larvae to small-size day geckos. The adult moths are also relished by many day geckos and can be rotated with crickets as a primary food source.

Wingless (vestigial-winged) fruit flies or Drosophila (*Drosophila melanogaster*)

These tiny insects are an ideal and easily cultured food source for newly hatched, small juveniles, and smaller species of day geckos. Be sure to put a small piece of papaya or banana into the lizard's enclosure with the fruit flies. The insects will remain on or around the fruit. Be certain to always obtain the flightless, captive-produced fruit flies, as they are no mess or bother. If wild fruit flies are used,

To raise vestigial winged (wingless) fruit flies requires small jars with paper lids, a paper towel inside each jar and a small amount of Formula 4-24 Instant Drosophila Medium Blue® (Carolina Biological Supply). Add a pinch of yeast, a little water and let the mass settle before adding flies. Photo by Dennis Sheridan.

your house will be inundated with these small flying insects. Starter cultures and instant *Drosophila* food are available through biological supply houses. Simply follow instructions, adding water and a little yeast. I have listed several suppliers.

Houseflies, green and blue bottle flies, and other "standard-size" flies

In the wild, day geckos consume many flying insects. Because flies are soft bodied, they make an excellent day gecko food in captivity. However, at least in North America, as of yet no entrepreneur has seen fit to breed flightless (vestigial-winged) standard-size flies (Hint, hint!). The solution to this problem is relatively simple and brings out a Gary Larson, *The Far Side*®, mentality that is present in many herpers. Acquire or make a butterfly net. Take a chicken bone or strip of meat and place it on a section of newspaper in the middle of your backyard. Go inside and relate to your significant other or some of your animals. A little later in the day, come back outside with your net. "Voila!" Flies! Place the net over the flies. Invert the top section of the net into a clear plastic bag. Tie the plastic bag off with a rubberband. Place the plastic bag in your refrigerator for a <u>short</u> period of time (less than a minute) until the flies appear inactive, and drop to the bottom of the bag. At this point, remove the bag from the refrigerator. Pour the flies onto a section of newspaper. Using a pair of scissors, cut one wing from each fly. Dump the flies into a plastic container to be fed out later. (Author's note: this method will probably not prove useful during the winter in colder climates).

Other food sources

Grasshoppers, if fed out in the <u>small juvenile stage</u>, can be a useful food supplement for larger *Phelsuma*. They are widely fed to mid- and large-size lizards in Europe, where they go under the common name "locust." However, as a result of U.S.D.A. regulations, these insects are not typically available commercially in the U.S., because they cannot be sent across state lines.

Superworms or giant mealworms *(Zophobas morio)* may also be fed, in the small juvenile stage or as just-molted white specimens, to larger species of day geckos on a supplemental basis. This food source was originally developed by Dutch herpetologist, Bert Langerwerf. These beetle larvae in appropriate sizes can be purchased from pet stores and distributors.

Chilean caterpillars or butterworms *(Chilecomodia moorei)* are thin, colorful, reddish or yellow caterpillars which look something like elongated wax worms. They are still not widely available but are increasingly being offered at reptile trade shows. Much like wax moth larvae, these caterpillars are probably best used as one component of a varied insect diet.

Cockroaches, including a number of species. Some of them, if they are of appropriate size, may be tried as a supplemental food source for day geckos. It is essential, however, to be certain that any cockroaches offered are free of pesticides.

Papaya, other fruit supplements, fruit baby food
Hatchling day geckos should have daily access to a slice of fresh, ripe papaya or other sliced fruit. If that is not available, offer a small amount of banana or peach baby food. A baby food mixture containing lory (parrot) nectar and a powdered vitamin/mineral supplement also works quite well. Larger juveniles and adult day geckos must be provided with fruit or nectar twice a week. Put this supplement in a dry area of the enclosure. Remove after a day unless the fruit is still fresh. Always remove any fruit, baby food, or nectar that no longer appears good or which has started to mildew.

Unsuitable food sources
As a general rule, the following types of invertebrates should not be offered to day geckos as food: spiders, beetles with hard outer wing casings, mealy bugs, and ants. Also, any prey item which looks too large probably is.

Vitamin/mineral supplementation
This is a critical aspect of the husbandry of day geckos. Without special attention to vitamin/mineral supplementation, successful breeding and rearing of day geckos usually will not be possible.

Of particular importance are vitamin D3 and calcium. Vitamin D3 is required for the effective absorption of calcium. Calcium is required for a number of metabolic functions and will be critical during the formation of the skeletal systems of rapidly growing juveniles and to allow female day geckos to form the calcareous shells of eggs.

There are two other critical factors when selecting vitamin/mineral supplements for day geckos. One is the calcium/phosphorus ratio. In order for calcium to be effectively absorbed, the recommended

Papaya may be the most ideal fruit supplement. A section which is diced may be fed twice weekly. Photo by Dennis Sheridan.

An adult Standing's day gecko licks fruit baby food from a clean flat plastic lid at the base of the enclosure. Baby food may be supplemented once to twice a week. It should be removed after several hours so it does not spoil. Photo by Dennis Sheridan.

calcium/phosphorus ratio in the diet of lizards is two to one (two parts calcium to one part phosphorus).

Another critical factor is the amount of vitamin A in commercial supplements. Recent studies by Dr. Larry Talent of Oklahoma State University suggest that too much vitamin A may impair the calcium metabolism of day geckos. It is recommended that one use supplements with low vitamin A content, striving through mixing of supplements to achieve a higher ratio of vitamin D3 to vitamin A, the reverse of what one finds in many products (Table on page 47). Refer to Metabolic bone disease under Diseases and Disorders for more information on this important topic.

When reading the labels of powdered reptile vitamin/mineral supplements on the market, one finds that most contain very high levels of vitamin A compared with vitamin D3. Nekton-Rep® has a high vitamin A content and an inadequate vitamin A to vitamin D3 ratio, to the extent that it is not recommended for day geckos. To minimize the possible negative effects of too much vitamin A, commercial vitamin supplements should be mixed with calcium supplements that

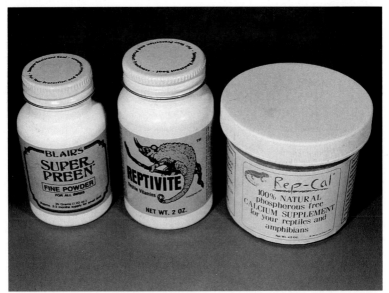

Super Preen®, Reptivite®, and Rep-Cal® are some of the commercially available powdered vitamin supplements used by keepers of day geckos. **Photo by Dennis Sheridan.**

have only vitamin D3 added, such as Reptical® or Nekton MSA®, which also contains other minerals. This procedure will increase the vitamin D3 to vitamin A ratio. It is also a good idea to feed crickets and other feeder insects intended for day geckos a low vitamin A diet, such as flaked baby cereals or ground rodent chow supplemented with powdered calcium carbonate.

The standard for supplementing insects with a powdered vitamin/mineral supplement is to place a small amount of supplement in a clear jar, introduce crickets, and gently swirl so that the crickets become coated before feeding them to the lizards.

An alternative method of supplementation and feeding is the use of semi-liquid diets. Nectars formulated for lories (nectar-feeding parrots) or Nekton Tonic®, when mixed as directed, will be valuable for day geckos if additional calcium/vitamin D3 supplements are added to offset an inappropriate vitamin A to vitamin D3 ratio. Liquid vitamins can be added to these commercial nectars. An alternative method used by many hobbyists is to offer banana or peach baby food mixed with vitamins and minerals. When rearing small day geckos, nectars or baby foods with vitamins will prove invaluable as a supplement, in addition to feeding small insects.

Supplementation schedules
The diets of adults should be supplemented two-to-three times a week. Juveniles should have their diet supplemented every one or two feedings.

Calcium carbonate
Many hobbyists leave a small, shallow dish of powdered calcium carbonate in their day gecko enclosures. The day geckos will eat or lick the calcium as the need arises. This needs to be protected from misting and should be replaced as it becomes contaminated.

Beware of ants! Ants will be attracted to any dead insects or to nectars and baby food. They can swarm and kill baby day geckos. Apply Vaseline® or other petroleum jelly to the outer sides of enclosures or place them on tables which have their legs sitting in cans of oil. Another method is to place the enclosures on bricks lying in trays of water. Heed this warning!

Breeding

Because of their exacting vitamin/mineral supplement requirements, particularly calcium and vitamin D3, day geckos require a high level of attention to their care in order to encourage consistent breeding over an extended period of time. If the reader is unable to provide a planted enclosure and meet the requirements as outlined in this manual, he/she may wish to purchase other animals, such as leopard geckos *(Eublepharis macularius)* or West African fat-tailed geckos *(Hemitheconyx caudicinctus),* for breeding and keep day geckos in vivaria individually, primarily for display.

However, if one is willing and able to provide the environmental conditions that day geckos need, a number of species will routinely breed in captivity. Among the larger forms, any of the *Phelsuma madagascariensis* group, as well as Standing's day gecko *(Phelsuma standingi),* will breed well in captivity. Among the smaller taxa, the gold dust day gecko *(Phelsuma laticauda)* and the dull day gecko *(Phelsuma dubia)* are relatively easy taxa to breed. Other forms are more difficult, but with effort and practice can be successfully captive bred. Additional data is provided in the species accounts, which will inform you as to the particular needs of each day gecko, based in large part on how and where it lives in the wild. What follows below is a generalized overview of day gecko management and care.

Setting up breeding groups
For the purpose of breeding, you will need to start with at least one sexually mature pair of a given species. The first step is to be certain to acquire correctly sexed animals. Without careful scrutiny, subadult or less dominant males may initially appear to be females.

Pre-breeding conditioning
Prior to breeding, all animals should be in good health and show proper body weight. Some breeders expose their lizards to a pre-breeding conditioning period, consisting of a shorter photoperiod, less than 12 hours of daylight in each 24 hour period, and cooler temperatures, such as 70°F (21°C) at night and 74-76°F (23-24°C) during the day, for six to ten weeks prior to peak breeding periods. If you are not having success without pre-breeding conditioning, then, using each species account, switch to a conditioning approach.

BREEDING METHODS
Housing as pairs
It is generally best to keep a pair of day geckos together all year. However,if the male seems too aggressive or the pair incompatible, then they will need to be separated and different, more compatible mates may need to be acquired.

Group breeding
Some taxa live in the wild in groups rather than pairs. With these, if the enclosure is sufficiently large and well planted, a male may be successfully housed with two or more females. The key is providing sufficient territory for each and to monitor each animal for signs of aggression. Aggression may be between the male and one of the females, or between females. In group housing, it is important that each of the females is of comparable size and that each has sufficient space. Never house two males together in the same enclosure, as serious aggression over territory may occur, resulting in injury to, or possibly the death of, one or both of the animals.

Breeding season
In the wild, most day geckos breed actively for at least several months per year. Peak breeding times are highlighted in the species accounts. Under ideal captive circumstances, females may lay eggs as frequently as every two to three weeks, and exceptional females may lay throughout the year. However, some species may lay only several clutches per year. In general, day geckos tend to lay eggs in cycles.

Breeding conditioning
Breeding imposes substantial energy and calcium demands on females. Breeding females should be offered food every other day and food items should be coated with a vitamin/mineral mix, such as the products discussed under Vitamin/mineral supplementation.

Egg clutches and laying
A female will produce a clutch of either one or two eggs per laying. The eggshell is calcareous in nature, that is, once dried, the outer shell becomes quite hard. Depending on both the individual female and the species, eggs are typically laid in a protected location, such as leaf joints of plants or under bark. Some day gecko breeders construct areas in the enclosure that make ideal egg-laying sites. A number of *Phelsuma* species are communal egg layers, and more than one female will deposit eggs at a prime location.

Incubation of eggs
"Gluers"

There are two suitable methods used for incubating day gecko eggs. For day geckos that are "gluers," affixing their eggs to a hard surface, the eggs must be incubated *in situ* (in place), as they will break or become damaged if an attempt is made to remove them. Mauritius and Reunion (Mascarene) day geckos are "gluers," as are several Madagascar/Comoro species including *P. dubia* and also, according to Wilhelm Henkel, *P. barbouri, P. flavigularis,* and *P. leiogaster.*

There are two basic requirements for eggs of "gluer" species of day geckos. First, if the eggs are laid on a hard surface, it will be necessary for the entire enclosure to be maintained in a room or other suitable area at temperatures between 78-85°F (26-29°C). Second, the eggs should be covered to maintain adequate air humidity levels. This can be accomplished by purchasing a preshaped piece of clear plastic that is approximately 1-2 in. (2.5-5 cm) long and 0.5-1 in. (1.3-2.5 cm) wide, depending on the relative size of the eggs. A correctly-shaped piece of plastic may often be a container for a commonly purchased item at a drug store, such as a plastic container for nails, screws, small picture hangers, or women's cosmetics. Remove the purchased item and the backing from the plastic container. With a push-pin or sewing needle, make a number of tiny air holes near the base. Next, cut out a very small section of paper towel. Fold it and place it in the bottom of the empty, clear plastic container. Fit the plastic container over the eggs, making certain it is deep enough so that it does not accidentally press against the eggs. Use sturdy tape or push pins to hold the plastic container in place over the eggs. Write the date in pencil below the egg clutch so you will know when the eggs were laid. Using lukewarm water in a spray bottle, lightly mist the paper towel at the base of the plastic container, through the tiny air holes on the lower portion, every other day. Use a fine spray in a manner that moistens, but does not saturate, the interior of the container.

If the eggs from a "gluer" species of day gecko are laid on a leaf, the section of leaf holding the eggs can be carefully cut out. During this process, be very careful to support the leaf or leaf joint with your hand from underneath, so that the eggs do not accidentally fall and break. The section of leaf with the eggs can then be transferred to an artificial incubation setup.

"Non-gluers"

If the species of day gecko is a "non-gluer," once the eggs have hardened, they can be carefully removed from virtually almost any surface so that they can be set up for artificial incubation. If you have a room or other area which remains in the high 70s to mid 80s°F (25-29°C), incubation of eggs is quite easy. Take an empty, plastic delicatessen, cottage cheese, or other container with a clear plastic top and thoroughly wash and rinse it out. Next, punch a series of tiny air holes in the lid with a push pin. Add 1-2 in. (2.5-5 cm) of slightly moistened fine vermiculite at a ratio of two parts vermiculite to one part water (by volume) to the bottom of the container. Some day gecko keepers have found that fine vermiculite does not dry out as quickly as the thick vermiculite. The exact degree of moisture, as long as it is not too moist or bone dry, is not critical if the correct medium is used. Moisten fine vermiculite in lukewarm water, squeeze it out in your cupped hand until it stops dripping, and then transfer the vermiculite to the bottom of the plastic container. Next, place a film canister lid or other small plastic lid on top of the vermiculite and place the eggs on that surface so that the eggs themselves are not sitting on the vermiculite. If the eggs are fertile, they should hatch

Madagascar giant day gecko eggs *in-situ* **at the base of bromeliad leaves. Photo by Ken T. Nemuras.**

Female giant day gecko laying egg in axil of *Sansevieria* **leaf, demonstrating the characteristic egg deposition behavior. Drawing by Glen Warren.**

in 38-90 days, depending on the taxa, and the temperatures used to incubate. If pushed to temperature-incubating extremes, such as a low of 73°F (23°C) or a high of 86°F (30°C), hatching times can vary from 31-128 days. Generally, a temperature that fluctuates between 77-84°F (25-29°C) is ideal for most species. This degree of fluctuation, while desirable, is not absolutely necessary.

A variation of the egg incubation technique just discussed is to purchase either a small styrofoam poultry egg incubator, such as a Hovabator®, or a small chick brooder enclosure. Set the temperature to 82°F (28°C) and place the covered plastic containers in the incubator or brooder. Change the settings slightly in each direction on a regular basis. The goal, of course, is to maintain the eggs at a relatively high humidity and at a suitable temperature so that incubation conditions which the eggs would experience in the wild are approximated. Unlike eggs from some terrestrial species of geckos, once dried, day gecko eggs are hard shelled and will not increase in size during the incubation process.

Other incubators that allow for the temperature and humidity requirements outlined are also quite suitable. For instance, if you breed a number of other reptiles, you may wish to construct a homemade incubator suitable for eggs from a variety of species. Purchase a submersible aquarium heater (a 75-100 watt model is suitable for smaller incubators). Place it at the bottom of an empty 20 gallon (76 liter) aquarium and add water to a height of 1-2 in. (2.5 - 5 cm) above the heater. Construct a sturdy platform several inches above the water level. Set your plastic containers on top of the platform. Be sure to include a label of masking tape on each plastic container showing the species, laying female, male parent, and date the eggs were laid. Finally, add a tight-fitting styrofoam cover, with a few holes punched through for ventilation over the top of the aquarium incubator.

Calibrating your incubator

Whether you are using a commercial or homemade incubator, calibration of the thermostat to the desired temperature or temperatures is critical. The key is to select a good-quality thermometer which should be placed inside the incubator. The best type for this purpose are the electronic thermometers with a thermal sensor. These are available in electronic supply stores. The cost varies between fifteen and thirty dollars depending on the features. The more expensive sensors should give a daily minimum and maximum temperature reading. Several models even have an alarm system that beeps to warn you if the temperature goes above or below a selected setting. To use these more high-tech models, place the sensor inside the incubating container and switch to the "out" reading. This will permit a constant monitoring of the temperature. As a back-up, a less expensive, but good quality, standard thermometer can be used on a weekly basis to verify the readings. Calibration of the incubator may, from time to time, require small adjustments of the thermostatic control. Once you have made the adjustments, let the incubator run awhile before proceeding with another adjustment. Typically, it takes several minutes for the temperature to settle to the new thermostatic adjustment. This process can take time and patience. Therefore, should you decide to use this method, prepare the incubator in advance of the eggs being laid. Proper calibration will prove critical to your hatching success.

Incubation temperatures

Recent preliminary studies by Brian Viets of Indiana University and Larry Talent of Oklahoma State University seem to indicate that the sex of day gecko eggs may be determined by incubation temperature.

Day gecko eggs inside an incubator. Each clutch is in a separate shallow plastic cup over moistened media. Incubation temperatures vary between 77-85°F (25-29°C). Photo by Jurriaan Schulman.

With a majority of day gecko species, if incubation temperatures are varied between 77 - 85°F (25 - 29°C), individuals of both sexes will be produced. However, certain species, including *Phelsuma guimbeaui* from Mauritius and *Phelsuma guntheri* from Round Island, when bred in captivity, produced almost exclusively females. The etiology of this heavily skewed sex distribution in favor of females under captive conditions has yet to be understood.

No matter what type of incubation set-up you choose, the incubating medium needs to be checked on a regular basis. If the vermiculite in the plastic containers seems to be drying out, a little lukewarm water can be added along the inside edges of the plastic container to bring up the moisture level. Some breeders prefer to use distilled or bottled water for this purpose.

Always be certain that the eggs are not placed directly on the medium, but rather on a flat plastic platform above the medium. It is essential that air humidity levels remain high. Most *Phelsuma* breeders prefer air humidity levels of over 75% for incubating eggs. If these levels drop too low, dead-in-shell syndrome will be high. On the other hand, if the eggs are permitted to become too wet, approaching 100% humidity, many of the potential neonates will go full term, but will die just before hatching. This may be due to drowning as the lizard begins the process of breaking out of the eggshell.

Raising neonates and juveniles
Neonate (newly hatched) day geckos break out of the egg by piercing it with a sharply pointed egg tooth at the tip of the snout. The egg tooth drops off shortly after hatching. Hatchling and small juvenile day geckos can be housed individually or in pairs, in 3-6 gallon (11.5-23 liters) vivaria. Commercially available plastic aquaria with a small, top center section which opens, available in pet shops, suit this purpose nicely. The species accounts in this book will tell you which juveniles will need to be housed singly. Each vivarium should have one or two small-to-medium-size potted plants. The lizard(s) can climb, lap water during misting, as well as rest on these plants, while basking under full-spectrum lighting. If any aggression is noted, or if there are skin rips or portions of tail missing from either of the individuals housed together, immediately remove that affected individual to its own, specially-set-up vivarium. Otherwise, it will continue to be stressed, and will probably die.

Hatchlings and juveniles of smaller forms should be fed pinhead-size, or small numbers of first stage, crickets and wingless fruit flies, which should be dusted with a vitamin/mineral supplement on a daily basis. Additionally, fresh fruit or a nectar mix should also be provided daily to neonates and every other day to larger juveniles. Misting parts of the enclosure with lukewarm water is required in the morning and early evening to provide the lizards with water. The plants in the enclosure will also need to be watered regularly. Juveniles of larger species of *Phelsuma* may be fed second or third stage crickets and small wax moth larvae using the same regime. Many day gecko breeders do not use water bowls as it is easy for insects to fall in and drown. A small rock in the water bowl may prevent this. Any water bowl used should be shallow to permit easy access. Add a drop of liquid vitamins to the water and change on a regular basis. Water is best supplemented by misting the plant and the walls of one side of the vivarium. Be sure to meticulously label each tank as to the date the eggs were laid, date of hatch, and specific parents of each offspring as this will allow you to genetically manage your lizards. Good record keeping will also enhance your opportunity to exchange or trade specimens with many other responsible breeders.

A newly hatched day gecko inside a clear plastic box housing several different egg clutches. The container lid, containing tiny air holes, has been removed to allow for the photo. This neonate is just out of the shell and has not yet shed. Photo by Jurriaan Schulman.

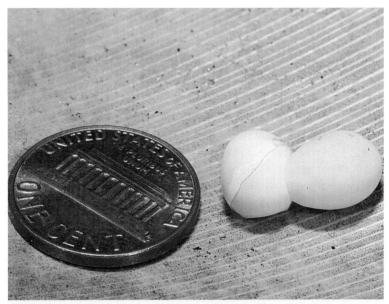

Eggs of *Phelsuma klemmeri.* This beautiful recently-described species has proven hardy and easy to propagate. Photo by Richard Bartlett ©1992.

Neonate Maruitius lowland forest day gecko *(Phelsuma guimbeaui guimbeaui).* Photo by the author.

Diseases and Disorders

When properly fed and maintained in a well-planted vivarium that is kept clean and has good air flow, day geckos are not prone to disease. Thus, prevention through good husbandry practice is the best way to avoid disease.

When obtaining day geckos, captive-bred specimens are preferable to wild-caught individuals for both conservation and health reasons. Always select a specimen that is alert, that will feed in front of you, and does not have sections of unshed skin stuck to any part of its body. The best way to monitor health is by a visual check of each lizard at least twice daily. Look at body posture and alertness. Look for a non-feeding response when food is offered. Look for any damage to the skin. Once you know what color repertoire a healthy specimen of a given species should have, stress coloration must be immediately addressed. This usually means checking the temperature and humidity gradients or looking for aggression between specimens. If there is aggression, this usually requires removing the stressed individual to its own separate enclosure. If any health problem is suspected, catch it early. Most wild animals, including day geckos, generally do not look "sick" until they are very ill.

If an imported *Phelsuma* seems dehydrated and appears to suffer from parasitism, Flagyl® can be dusted onto baby food with favorable results. Of course, any medication should only be used as directed by a qualified reptile veterinarian. In general, because of the small size and high stress factor of these lizards, if an antibiotic is prescribed, an oral antibiotic is strongly preferred over an injectable one.

Vitamin/mineral requirements and metabolic bone disease

This condition is most frequently seen in female and juvenile day geckos which have been fed a diet of commercially-raised insects without dietary supplements. A diet lacking the proper 2:1 calcium to phosphorus ratio and vitamin D3 may result in improper bone development, even if the necessary full-spectrum lighting is used. Symptoms of metabolic bone disease are usually indicated by a soft, flexible lower jaw, some deformation of the limbs, a kinked tail, the inability to climb well and if stressed, seizures. This condition, if caught early enough, can be corrected through improving the habitat/living conditions and proper insect "dusting" with a powdered vitamin/mineral supplement.

Over the last two years, Dr. Larry Talent of the Department of Zoology at Oklahoma State University has conducted preliminary experiments on several species of day geckos to better understand some of their nutritional requirements. Most of his work has been on *Phelsuma madagascariensis grandis* and is directed toward the development of an artificial diet. Dr. Talent's most significant findings of interest to breeders and hobbyists are that two vitamins, A and D, are responsible for many of the nutrition-related health problems sometimes encountered with captive day geckos.

A deficiency of vitamin D3 causes metabolic bone disease. A kinked back just anterior to the hind legs resulting in full or partial paralysis of the hind legs is sometimes the first symptom of a vitamin D deficiency. Another symptom is rickets, which may be first noticed in the lizard having difficulty climbing vertical surfaces. Kinked tails may also develop, particularly in those lizards that alternate between receiving too little D3 and adequate amounts of the vitamin.

An overdose of vitamin D3 results in a number of problems as well. Some *Phelsuma* receiving a mild-to-moderate overdose of vitamin D3 may have difficulty shedding, particularly on the head and toes. The outer layer of skin may become flaky and brittle, preventing the lizards from removing it. Surprisingly, severe overdosing with vitamin D3 can also result in tail kinking and kinking of the spine, the very symptoms produced by too little vitamin D3, but typically without hind limb paralysis.

An excess of vitamin A also results in major health problems in day geckos, as it can cause decalcification of the skeleton. Metabolic bone disease can result from either an underdose of vitamin D3, an overdose of vitamin A, or both, assuming the lizard is receiving adequate amounts of minerals such as calcium. Skeletal degeneration can also be caused by calcium deficiency in the diet. If a lizard has metabolic bone disease, do not assume that it needs more vitamin supplementation in general. If the cause is an overdose of vitamin A, then more supplementation with a complete vitamin mix could make the problem worse. Regardless of the cause of metabolic bone disease, the symptoms can be reversed, in most case by increasing vitamin D3 supplementation and providing extra calcium and other minerals. In these cases, vitamin A supplementation should be held constant or decreased. For more advanced cases, placing a drop of liquid calcium carbonate onto the lizard's snout daily, using an eye dropper, may be helpful if the lizard will cooperate by licking the fluid. It may also be helpful to put liquid vitamins with a low vitamin A to vitamin D3 ratio in the water used for misting or drinking.

Dr. Talent's research is ongoing. He is in the process of sorting out questions of vitamin requirements and tolerances. It appears from his work that day geckos can tolerate a range of vitamins. However, those receiving high levels of vitamin A need considerably more vitamin D3 than lizards receiving less vitamin A, so keep the amount of vitamin A low.

Unfortunately, at present the American market does not offer any product which meets the specific vitamin/mineral requirements of most day geckos. Until someone comes up with an artificial diet or an additive with the proper balance, the best results can probably be obtained by mixing several of the reptile vitamin/mineral supplements together. In making your selection, read product labels carefully. Until more information becomes available, work towards supplementing vitamin D to vitamin A at a ratio nearing 1 to 1; that is, one part vitamin D3 to one part vitamin A. If you also use additional calcium, be sure it is pure calcium carbonate or calcium gluconate, or a mix with at least two parts calcium to one part phosphorus.

FEED AND SUPPLEMENT CONCENTRATIONS OF PREFORMED VITAMIN A

SUPPLEMENT / FEED	VITAMIN A CONCENTRATION	FORM OF RETINYL ESTER	APPROX. No. OF DUSTED ADULT CRICKETS TO EQUAL 250 IU	VITAMIN D_3 CONCENTRATION	Ratio Of Vitamin A To D_3
NEKTON-REP®	6,600 IU/gm	Retinyl Palmitate	1.6 ▲	10 IU/gm	660
VitaFlight®	3,960 IU/gm	Retinyl Palmitate	2.7	1,975 IU/gm	2
Vitalife®	2,203 IU/gm	Retinyl Palmitate	4.9	114 IU/gm	19
Super-Preen®	1,982 IU/gm	Retinyl Acetate	5.5	114 IU/gm	17
OsteoForm®	360 IU/gm	Retinyl Acetate	30.1	36 IU/gm	10
VIONATE®	220 IU/gm	Retinyl Palmitate	49.2 ▼	22 IU/gm	10
REPTIVITE®	220 IU/gm	Retinyl Palmitate	49.2	23 IU/gm	9
INJACOM-100®	100,000 IU/cc	Retinyl Palmitate	Not Applicable	10,000 IU/cc	10
Vita-Sol®	10,651 IU/cc	Retinyl Palmitate	Not Applicable	2,282 IU/cc	5
Avitron®	1,041 IU/cc	Retinyl Palmitate	Not Applicable	156 IU/cc	7
Chicken Starter	27 IU/gm	Retinyl Acetate	Not Applicable	6 IU/gm	4
Cricket Feed	9-12 IU/gm	Retinyl Acetate	Not Applicable	1+ IU/gm	9+
Pure Preformed Vitamin A	~1 Million IU/gm ▲	Retinyl Palmitate	Not Applicable	Not Applicable	Not Applicable

▲Crickets Were Misted With Water To Enhance Supplement Adhesion, ▼Calculated Based On Reptivite Cricket Weight Delta

▲Concentration Varies With Each Production Batch Run Of Retinyl Palmitate

Courtesy of John Annis and Chameleon Information Network (C.I.N.).

Finally, be certain your vitamin/mineral supplements are fresh. Check the expiration date on the container. Keep the top on the container when not in use. Many fat soluble vitamins oxidize rapidly.

Unfiltered, natural sunlight is very helpful in allowing lizards to process vitamin D3. Maintenance in large, outdoor, screened enclosures affording areas of both sun and shade during the warmer months of the year will significantly lessen the occurrence of metabolic bone disease.

Shedding problems
Incomplete shedding is characterized by parts of unshed skin remaining attached to the body or extremities, especially the toe pads. If ignored, this problem will quickly lead to the inability to climb vertical surfaces, loss of digits, or if the skin is on the caudal appendage, the loss of a distal portion of tail, and may even result in the death of the lizard. Do not let this condition go unattended.

The principal cause is lack of proper humidity. After a day gecko has finished shedding, observe whether portions of unshed, outer-layer skin remain. Repeated light misting of those areas with lukewarm water may enable the gecko to pull off any remaining skin with its jaws. If this does not work, the lizard may need to be gently but firmly grabbed and, after misting the digits, the excess shed removed with a pair of tweezers. Use the tweezers only on unshed outer skin, not a section of the digit underneath, or major damage could occur.

If incomplete sheddings happen regularly, it probably indicates that the humidity in the enclosure is too low. This problem can usually be corrected by placing additional potted plants in the enclosure along with more frequent misting. A problem shed may also result from too cool or too warm an enclosure temperature and/or improper vitamin/mineral supplementation. If the problem persists, review your overall management.

Another cause of shedding problems is illness. Weak animals or animals with calcium deficiency will not be able to shed their skins. Any animal on the bottom of the enclosure which is having problems shedding may be ill and should be examined and treated. Loose shed skin may have to be manually removed.

Dermal and digit infections
If maintained in a vivarium that is too moist and/or dirty, day geckos may develop serious skin infections which may lead to more exten-

sive damage and/or to loss of digits. First, immediately rectify the associated cause. Be certain the substrate is not too moist or fouled. If necessary, substitute a temporary dry, clean substrate such as newspaper. Treat superficial infections with a topical antibiotic ointment such as Neosporin® or a generic equivalent. If additional antibiotic therapy is necessary, this will require the attention of an experienced reptile veterinarian. If you don't have a good reptile veterinarian, your regional zoo reptile house can probably recommend one.

Stomatitis or mouth rot

If this disease is seen at all in day geckos, it is usually with newly imported specimens, improperly housed in screened enclosures, where they rub their noses on the screen. The identifying symptom is a raw-appearing or discolored snout. If the damage is relatively minor, apply a topical antibiotic such as Neosporin® with a cotton swab. If the condition does not clear up within a week or worsens, immediately consult a reptile veterinarian for an oral antibiotic.

Respiratory infections

Respiratory infections are uncommon in captive day geckos. Improper enclosure temperature, especially too cool an enclosure temperature, increases susceptibility. Partial opening of the mouth when resting, or labored exhalation are the most typical symptoms in geckos. Should you suspect a respiratory infection, it is important to immediately raise the daytime temperature to 84-88°F (29-31°C) with a drop at night not below 80°F (27°C). If significant improvement is not noticeable within a week, or if the condition worsens, see a reptile veterinarian for a positive diagnosis and antibiotics.

Gastroenteritis/loose stools

The most obvious sign of a gastroenteric disease is substantial weight loss combined with the passing of watery or bloody stools. There may also be a loss of appetite and some degree of listlessness. An immediate course of action is needed. Arrange to take a fresh stool sample to a reptile veterinarian to have a stool check/culture performed to determine the cause. If necessary, the veterinarian can recommend a safe antibiotic to which the causal organisms are susceptible. If properly treated and if the environmental conditions are suitable, the lizard should quickly return to good health. If untreated, infections of the digestive tract are often fatal. Flagellate protozoans are one cause of gastroenteritis. If flagellates are found, the recommended treatment is to administer Flagyl® (metronidazole) orally at a dosage of 100 mg/kg. Several types of worms also cause gastroenteritis and may be treated by the veterinarian with one of several relatively safe dewormers such as Panacur®.

Gravel/sand impaction

This condition is rare in arboreal geckos and is typically due to improper housing and/or food supplementation. Never house day geckos on gravel or sand. Feed baby food or sliced fruit in a shallow plastic tray, lid, or on a flat discardable cardboard surface. Also, provide access to calcium carbonate in a shallow container at an elevated location. The symptoms of substrate impaction are a lethargic animal which spends too much time on the floor of the enclosure. If the lizard is handled, the sand or gravel can be felt through the skin of the gut area. In such an instance, immediately change the improper substrate and hope that most of the impacted material will gradually pass with defecations.

Missing tail

A missing tail indicates either fighting with an enclosure mate or careless handling. This is not an act without consequences because the lizard is losing some of its fat reserves. If fighting with a conspecific is suspected, the lizard should be removed from the enclosure and housed singly under optimal conditions until it regenerates a new tail. While separated, the tailless day gecko must also be placed in a suitable-size enclosure under full-spectrum lighting, kept warm, and be fed and misted regularly.

Small patches of ripped skin

This almost always indicates aggression between enclosure mates and, if not dealt with immediately, can quickly result in life threatening stress and death of the affected lizard(s). Always observe your lizards carefully on a daily basis. If damaged skin areas are noted, immediately separate the lizards and set up the damaged animal in its own enclosure under optimal conditions. Next, look carefully at each specimen and determine if one of the lizards may have been incorrectly sexed (male geckos should never be housed together). If you are sure that the animals involved are a sexual pair or two females, you will need to wait until both animals are fully recovered before any reintroduction is attempted. You will also need to acquire a considerably larger enclosure with more live plants in order to afford each lizard its own territory and necessary shelters.

SPECIES ACCOUNTS
Phelsuma abbotti

SCIENTIFIC NAME: *Phelsuma abbotti abbotti*

COMMON NAME: Aldabra Island day gecko

WHO DESCRIBED TAXON AND WHEN: Stejneger, 1893.

TOTAL LENGTH: An average snout-vent length of 2.25 in. (56 mm) in males and 2 in. (52 mm) in females. Reaches a total length of 4.25 - 5 in. (10.8 - 12.7 cm) for Aldabra populations. Individual specimens from Madagascar are larger, reaching a total length of 5.5 in. (14.0 cm). Hatchlings of Madagascar *P. a. abbotti* are 1.75 in. (4.5 cm) in length.

DISTRIBUTION: Found on Aldabra Atoll, one of several low islands north of Madagascar, which are part of the Republic of the Seychelles, although far to the south of the granitic Seychelles. Also found in northern Madagascar and on the small offshore island of Nosy Be.

TYPICAL HABITAT: On Aldabra, stunted low trees and bushes. Lives on native mixed scrub and *Pemphis* thickets and on introduced coconut trees. As with other Seychelles *Phelsuma*, it does not utilize mangrove trees or *Casuarina*. On Nosy Be, it lives on coastal, pantropic vegetation.

BRIEF DESCRIPTION: A small species with a charcoal-colored eye stripe that extends from the tip of the snout down to the neck region. Lacks brilliant color; shades are more pastel in appearance. Above, light grayish blue when active and dull greenish gray when inactive. Typically, a thin charcoal-colored mid-dorsal stripe is present. A series of charcoal-colored spots, dots, lines, and bars are present on the flanks, tail, and legs. Will occasionally climb onto giant tortoises to groom them of external parasites. In general, there is little opportunity to feed on nectar, and in the wild, this taxon is almost exclusively insectivorous.

MANAGEMENT AND CAPTIVE BREEDING: Does well in captivity. Requires typical lowland coastal day gecko management with live plants. Care for in a manner similar to *P. laticauda*.

SCIENTIFIC NAME: *Phelsuma abbotti sumptio*

COMMON NAME: Assumption Island day gecko

WHO DESCRIBED TAXON AND WHEN: Cheke, 1982.

TOTAL LENGTH: Males average 2.75-3 in. (72-75 mm) snout-vent length while females average 2.6-2.75 in. (65-67.5 mm). This lizard reaches a total length of 5.5-6 in. (14-15.2 cm) and is significantly larger than *P. a. abbotti* on Aldabra.

DISTRIBUTION: Assumption Island, a high atoll located in the same grouping of islands as Aldabra and a part of the Seychelles, although many hundreds of miles south of the granitic Seychelles.

TYPICAL HABITAT: Palms, introduced vegetation, and bushes.

BRIEF DESCRIPTION: Dorsally sky blue when in peak activity, varying to grayish blue when inactive. Skin colors are more pastel or subdued. A thin rust-colored eye stripe is present between nostril and eye. A series of rust-colored dots and lines are present on the head. A thin broken mid-dorsal rust-colored stripe is bordered by irregular spotting. Ventrally, skin color is white. The femoral pores in males are well developed.

MANAGEMENT AND BREEDING IN CAPTIVITY: Manage as you would *P. a. abbotti.*

Abbott's day gecko *(Phelsuma a. abbotti)* occurs in northern Madagascar, the offshore islet of Nosy Be, and on the island of Aldabra. Photo by the author.

Phelsuma andamanensis

SCIENTIFIC NAME: *Phelsuma andamanensis*

COMMON NAME: Andaman Islands day gecko

WHO DESCRIBED TAXON AND WHEN: Blyth, 1860.

TOTAL LENGTH: A small to mid-size species averaging 4.5-6 in. (11.4-15.4 cm).

DISTRIBUTION: Confined to the Andaman Islands where it has wide distribution. These islands are located in the Bay of Bengal, at a considerable distance from the western Indian Ocean islands habitat of other *Phelsuma*.

TYPICAL HABITAT: Found on palms, including coconut palms, and other tropical vegetation at low elevation. Commonly found in domestic gardens. Individuals utilize overlapping home ranges. Breeding and egg laying occur throughout the year. Typically lays two eggs in a protected, elevated location. The undersurfaces of palm fronds are favored locations for egg laying. Greatest species densities are on coconut plantations.

BRIEF DESCRIPTION: In males, the body is bright green and the tail is bluish green. Females are uniformly green. The snout is long and pointed, with a reddish brown v-shaped nose stripe extending from the nostril past the eye. Reddish brown spots are present on the back of the head. Smaller spots continue down the middle of the back, becoming larger on the lower back, forming a small cluster above the rear legs. The limbs are a dull greenish gray. The underside of the chin is yellow. The undersurface of the body is off-white.

MANAGEMENT AND BREEDING IN CAPTIVITY: Since this is a generalized lowland form which lives in groups on palms and garden vegetation, it should be managed similar to other comparable species, such as *P. astriata*. This taxon has not been imported into the United States to date.

An Andaman Islands day gecko *(Phelsuma andamanensis)*. Photo by Rom Whitaker.

Phelsuma astriata

SCIENTIFIC NAME: *Phelsuma astriata astriata*

COMMON NAME: Seychelles small day gecko

WHO DESCRIBED TAXON AND WHEN: Tornier, 1901.

TOTAL LENGTH: 4.5-5.5 in. (11.4 - 14 cm).

DISTRIBUTION: Occurs on the southwestern granitic islands of the Seychelles, including the large island of Mahé.

TYPICAL HABITAT: Common in some areas on coconut trees. Also very common in introduced pantropic vegetation, such as small palms, bananas, papayas, in gardens and vegetation bordering human dwellings.

BRIEF DESCRIPTION: A thin-bodied, smallish day gecko that is lime green in color. A thin rust-colored line extends from the nostril to below the eye. A rust-colored spot may be present on the top of the head. Irregular rust-colored spots and bars are present on the back and tail. Typically, the mid-dorsal stripe is either lacking or very faint. A light blue hue is sometimes present on the lower back and upper portion of the tail. Ventral surface is off-white. Will colony nest (a number of females utilizing the same nesting location) where ideal nesting sites occur. Such locations may include holes in the trunks of trees or under protected places on human dwellings.

MANAGEMENT AND BREEDING IN CAPTIVITY: House as sexual pairs in a well-planted, vertically-oriented vivarium. Bromeliads and *Dracaena* are plants that work well. Feed adults one week old crickets and supplement with other small insects. Also offer fruit, fruit baby food, or Necton Tonic R®, once-to-twice weekly. Remove eggs from the protected location in which they were laid and incubate at 82°F (28°C) plus or minus 2°F; incubation period is 61-68 days.

A close-up of *Phelsuma astriata semicarinata,* showing relative size. This species is native to the granitic islands of the Seychelles, approximately 1,000 miles north of Madagascar. Photo by the author.

Phelsuma astriata, like other members of the genus, feeds on nectar and pollen and, in so doing, helps to pollinate many endemic plants including orchids and palms. Photo by the author.

SCIENTIFIC NAME: *Phelsuma astriata semicarinata*

COMMON NAME: None

WHO DESCRIBED TAXON AND WHEN: Cheke, 1976.

TOTAL LENGTH: Males have an average snout to vent length of 2.4 in. (61 mm) while females average 2.25-2.75 in. (56-68 mm). Average total length is 4.5-5.5 in. (11.4-14 cm); neonates average slightly over 1.5 in. (4 cm).

DISTRIBUTION: Occurs in the eastern granitic islands of the Seychelles, including Praslin and Curieuse.

TYPICAL HABITAT: This subspecies utilizes a wide range of vegetation at lower and mid-elevations. However, because of the presence of the much larger *P. sundbergi* on mature coconut trees and coco-de-mer palms, resource partitioning occurs between the two forms, as the former will pursue and attempt to eat the latter. *P. astriata* is present on immature coconut palms, other small palms, coastal hardwood trees, and pantropic vegetation in gardens and around dwellings. Density levels are high in suitable environments.

BRIEF DESCRIPTION: A thin-bodied, smallish day gecko. The snout is long with a rust-colored line between the nostril and the eye and an inverted v-shaped, rust-colored marking extending from mid-snout to behind the eye. A thin mid-dorsal stripe is present. The stripe may be broken and may have a series of bars extending from it. The dorsal surface has irregular-shaped bars and spots. Females sometimes utilize communal nest sites in the wild. These are often under bark or in tree cavities. This taxon is somewhat varied in appearance from island to island. They feed on insects, fruits, nectar, and pollen.

MANAGEMENT AND BREEDING IN CAPTIVITY: Manage in a manner similar to *P. a . astriata.*

Phelsuma barbouri

SCIENTIFIC NAME: *Phelsuma barbouri*

COMMON NAME: Barbour's day gecko

WHO DESCRIBED TAXON AND WHEN: Loveridge, 1942.

TOTAL LENGTH: A small-size yet robust species, growing to an average length of 4.5-5 in. (11.4-12.7 cm), with large individuals achieving a length of 5.4 in. (135 mm).

DISTRIBUTION: Central Madagascar, including the region around Tsiafojavona in the Ankaratra Mountains, at relatively high elevation. This region reaches a maximum daytime temperature of 86°F (30°C). At night, it is cool and foggy.

TYPICAL HABITAT: Unlike other *Phelsuma*, this species lives on the ground or on rocks. It is found in places that are rocky with some short grasses and small plants present.

Barbour's day gecko *(Phelsuma barbouri).* Photo by R.D. Bartlett.

BRIEF DESCRIPTION: A somewhat somber-colored day gecko with a head that is more or less brownish or greenish brown with some charcoal-colored markings. The body is dark green or brownish green. A wide, dark brown dorso-lateral stripe extends from head to tail, bordered on its lower portion by a light green stripe. Another dark brown stripe extends the length of the flank. The legs and feet are brown. The tail is greenish with some small dark spotting.

MANAGEMENT AND BREEDING IN CAPTIVITY: This species must be housed very differently from other day geckos. Maintain in an earth-based vivarium, with a number of flat rocks present. A group of rocks at one end laid on top of one another in a graduated manner will provide a sturdy base for climbing. Include small plants that grow along the ground to provide a little cover. Daytime temperatures may be in the 84-86°F (29°C) range with a nighttime drop to 68-70°F (20.5°C). House in sexual pairs. Two eggs are typically laid under stones. Once laid, they should be removed and incubated in a manner similar to other day gecko eggs. When incubated at 78-82°F (26-28°C), the eggs typically hatch between 51-55 days, and neonates are 1-1.25 in. (3.2 cm) in length.

Phelsuma beaufotakensis

SCIENTIFIC NAME: *Phelsuma beufotakensis*

COMMON NAME: None

WHO DESCRIBED THE TAXON AND WHEN: Borner, 1982.

TOTAL LENGTH: Averages 4-4.75 in. (10.2-12.1 cm).

DISTRIBUTION: Occurs along the northwest coast of Madagascar in the general region of Analalava near Befotaka.

TYPICAL HABITAT: This area has many small inlets and bays and is sheltered from cyclones. Originally, the vegetation consisted of tropical mixed forest although almost none of this remains. The region is characterized by a wet/dry season, with June through August being the driest months. This lizard typically occurs on secondary vegetation.

MANAGEMENT AND BREEDING IN CAPTIVITY: To date, this species has not been imported into the United States.

Phelsuma bimaculata

SCIENTIFIC NAME: *Phelsuma bimaculata*

COMMON NAME: None

WHO DESCRIBED THE TAXON AND WHEN: Kaudern, 1922. Until relatively recently, considered a subspecies of *P. quadriocellata.*

TOTAL LENGTH: Males average 4.25-5 in.(10.8-12.7 cm) and females 3.25-4 in. (8.3-10.2 cm).

DISTRIBUTION: The islet of Ste. Marie and the eastern coast of Madagascar.

TYPICAL HABITAT: This is a forest species living on big trees by rivers. Its use of riparian habitat is not unlike *P. g. guimbeaui* on Mauritius. On the main island, it is found on bushes near rivers, and on Ste. Marie, it is widely distributed in the forest on traveler palms, and on human dwellings.

BRIEF DESCRIPTION: A greenish gecko with a very distinctive dark red mark on the side of the body behind the front legs. Femoral pores are enlarged and reduced in number.

MANAGEMENT AND BREEDING IN CAPTIVITY: Rarely exported and has not, as yet, been imported into the United States. Manage in a well-planted vivarium with a single male and several females. The females tend to be shy, and require lots of planting and hiding spots. Eggs are typically laid in bamboo stalks. This species has bred well in captivity in the few European collections containing these lizards.

A male Agalega Island day gecko *(Phelsuma borbonica agalegae)*. Photo by Eddy Postma.

Phelsuma borbonica

SCIENTIFIC NAME: *Phelsuma borbonica borbonica*

COMMON NAME: Reunion Island day gecko

WHO DESCRIBED THE TAXON AND WHEN: Mertens, 1966.

TOTAL LENGTH: 4.5-6.5 in. (11.4-16.5 cm).

DISTRIBUTION: Mid elevation on Reunion, including the region around Le Brule, Ste. Marie, and Ste. Suzanne.

TYPICAL HABITAT: A low-density species, sometimes found on *Eugenia*. Often utilizes suburban backyard vegetation and fencing.

BRIEF DESCRIPTION: An attractive bluish green, pastel-colored lizard. The head is yellowish, finely mottled with brown. Two light dorso-lateral stripes extend from behind the eye to the base of the tail. A network of reticulated reddish bars are present on the back and tail. The sides of the body and legs are spotted. The ventral surface is yellowish with brown marbling.

MANAGEMENT AND BREEDING IN CAPTIVITY: House in planted vivaria. Prefers daytime highs of mid 80s°F (28-31°C) and nighttime lows in the high 60s to low 70s°F (19-22°C). House in pairs. Rare in American and European collections.

Reunion Island day gecko *(Phelsuma b. borbonica)*. A taxon rarely imported into the United States. Photo by Jurriaan Schulman.

SCIENTIFIC NAME: *Phelsuma borbonica agalegae*

COMMON NAME: Agalega Island day gecko

WHO DESCRIBED THE TAXON AND WHEN: Cheke, 1975.

TOTAL LENGTH: A mid-size day gecko, averaging 5-6.5 in. (12.7-16.5 cm).

DISTRIBUTION: Occurs only on Agalega, which is comprised of two small, low coral sand islands surrounded by an active reef. These islands are separated from each other by slightly less than one mile (1.5 km) of reef. Agalega is located 432 miles (685 km) northeast of Madagascar and is far closer to the granitic Seychelles (350 miles/564 km) than to Reunion (675 miles/1087 km). The island is administered by the government of Mauritius.

TYPICAL HABITAT: Widely distributed on coconut palms and accompanying broadleaf trees such as *Terminalia* and mango. Females often lay eggs communally under loose bark of coconut trees.

BRIEF DESCRIPTION: The colors on this lizard are not intense; they are more pastel shades. Males are slightly larger than females and are buff-colored, with a network of small reddish brown dots on the dorsal surface and tail. Females have a light brown head and body. The back has a network pattern of light blue bars and irregular-shaped dots. The tail is light blue with light brown barring. The flanks on both male and female are light gray or beige. Both have a light blue or greenish bar across the snout. Lizards leave their protected night hiding places under bark or at the base of fronds shortly after sunrise (6 a.m.), bask, and then search for food. Temperatures during the middle of the day (11 a.m.-4 p.m.) are quite hot, usually in excess of 90°F (32°C), and during this period the lizards retreat to protected areas. Foraging resumes in the late afternoon for an hour or so, before the lizards return to their protected night resting spots.

MANAGEMENT AND BREEDING IN CAPTIVITY: A generalized coastal lowland form that prefers mid 80s°F (28-31°C) during the day and nighttime temperatures in the mid 70s°F (23-26°C). Rarely exported and uncommon in captivity.

A *Phelsuma breviceps* from south of Tsiombe, Madagascar. Photo by R.A. Nussbaum.

Phelsuma breviceps

SCIENTIFIC NAME: *Phelsuma breviceps*

COMMON NAME: None

WHO DESCRIBED THE TAXON AND WHEN: Boettger, 1894.

TOTAL LENGTH: A very small species, growing to only 3-3.5 in. (7.6-8.9 cm).

DISTRIBUTION: S.E. Madagascar, including the region around Fort Dauphin.

TYPICAL HABITAT: Lives individually on dwellings and on bamboo corrals for cattle. The areas that it lives in are very hot and dry during the day, with nighttime temperatures of 59-63°F (15-17°C). Extremely wary, this species is typically only active in the early morning.

BRIEF DESCRIPTION: Light gray in color with pastel blue spotting.

MANAGEMENT AND BREEDING IN CAPTIVITY: Has not as yet been imported into the United States and the author does not know of any individuals in captivity in Europe.

Phelsuma cepediana

SCIENTIFIC NAME: *Phelsuma cepediana*

COMMON NAME: Blue-tailed day gecko

WHO DESCRIBED THE TAXON AND WHEN: Merrem, 1820.

TOTAL LENGTH: Males average 4.5-5.5 in. (11.4-14 cm) with large specimens reaching 6 in. (15.2 cm); females average 3.75-4.5 in. (9.5-11.4 cm).

DISTRIBUTION: Widely distributed in Mauritius, both coastal areas and interior regions, at low, mid, and high elevations. Adapts well to areas disturbed by humans, as long as some vegetation is present. Prefers less arid areas. Introduced in the region of Ivoloina, on the east coast of Madagascar in 1962.

TYPICAL HABITAT: Within the past 400 years, most of the natural vegetation on Mauritius has been destroyed and replaced with agricultural crops, such as sugar cane. Day geckos cannot live in these agricultural areas. *P. cepediana* is found on trees and bushes, including coconut palms, bananas, papayas, and traveler's palms. Healthy populations occur on bananas and other backyard vegetation in suburban areas of some villages and towns. Found in very high densities in suitable habitat where there is high rainfall or sufficient moisture.

BRIEF DESCRIPTION: A brilliantly-colored, sexually dimorphic species. When at peak activity colors, males are typically brilliant blue above with large, irregular red spots and dashes. A dorso-lateral stripe, which may or may not be broken, is always present. A red eye stripe extends from the back of the nostril to the shoulder. The flanks are a bright chartreuse. The tail is deep blue. Females are bright green with rust-colored spotting. A rust-colored dorso-lateral stripe and characteristic eye stripe are always present. Females from the upland populations frequently have brighter reds, reduced striping, and may have a cluster of small red spots on the lower back.

MANAGEMENT AND BREEDING IN CAPTIVITY: Females are extremely delicate and this species is best managed in vertically-oriented enclosures with live plants such as potted banana trees, *Dracaena,* bromeliads, philodendra, or birds of paradise. It is essential to use a well-planted enclosure with this species, and to keep

A male blue-tailed day gecko *(Phelsuma cepediana)* showing relative size.
Photo by the author.

A female blue-tailed day gecko *(Phelsuma cepediana)*. This is a delicate species only suited
for the most experienced and knowledgeable *Phelsuma* specialist. Photo by the author.

humidity levels up while affording sufficient air flow. This is accomplished through watering and heavy misting of major portions of the enclosure twice daily. House as pairs. This and other delicate day gecko species do much better if housed in screened outdoor enclosures with large potted plants during late spring, summer, and early fall when the temperatures are in the 70-90°F (21-32°C) range. Be sure there are areas which afford both sun and shade in these enclosures. This species is an "egg gluer." Manage neonates in a manner similar to *P. g. guimbeaui.*

An upland *Phelsuma cepediana.* Females from high elevation populations sometimes lack body striping and have a cluster of red dots on the lower back Photo by the author.

Phelsuma comorensis

SCIENTIFIC NAME: *Phelsuma comorensis*

COMMON NAME: None

WHO DESCRIBED THE TAXON AND WHEN: Boettger, 1913.

TOTAL LENGTH: Averages 4.5 in. (11.4 cm).

DISTRIBUTION: Grand Comoro Island in the Comoros.

TYPICAL HABITAT: Pantropic vegetation.

BRIEF DESCRIPTION: Pale green in color with some reddish brown dotting.

MANAGEMENT AND BREEDING IN CAPTIVITY: Manage similar to *P. laticauda*. Eggs typically hatch in 33-45 days when incubated at 82°F (28°C) plus or minus 2°F (1°C).

Phelsuma comorensis, a small species from the Comoro Islands. Photo by John Tashjian at Tim Tytle's breeding facility.

Phelsuma dubia

SCIENTIFIC NAME: *Phelsuma dubia*

COMMON NAME: Dull day gecko

WHO DESCRIBED THE TAXON AND WHEN: Boettger, 1881.

TOTAL LENGTH: A small-size species averaging 4-5 in. (10.2-12.7 cm).

DISTRIBUTION: Found on the western coast of Madagascar in the general area of Majunga; also, in the Comoros, in Zanzibar, and some coastal areas of mainland Tanzania. This species is thought to have been introduced by humans to the African mainland.

TYPICAL HABITAT: Lowland pantropic vegetation.

BRIEF DESCRIPTION: One of the least colorful of the day geckos. The dorsal surface is grayish green or grayish brown, sometimes with small, faint, irregular, greenish spotting; ventral surface is off-white. In the wild, eggs are often laid between dry banana leaves.

MANAGEMENT AND BREEDING IN CAPTIVITY: Manage in a manner similar to other lowland coastal forms, such as *P. laticauda.* However, *P. dubia* is an "egg gluer;" that is, the eggs adhere to the surface on which they are laid, and will become damaged if an attempt is made to move them. If laid on the glass or wall of an enclosure, they will need to be incubated *in situ.*

Phelsuma dubia, a species that generally lacks brilliant colors, and is often referred to by American hobbyists as the "dull" or "dull-colored" day gecko. Photo by R.D. Bartlett.

Three preserved specimens of the Rodrigues Island day gecko *(Phelsuma edwardnewtonii)* at the British Museum.

Phelsuma edwardnewtonii

SCIENTIFIC NAME: *Phelsuma edwardnewtonii*

COMMON NAME: Rodrigues day gecko

WHO DESCRIBED THE TAXON AND WHEN: Lienard, 1842.

TOTAL LENGTH: Reached a known length of 7.5-9 in. (19.1-22.9 cm), although one historical account places the maximum length at up to 10.6 in. (27 cm).

DISTRIBUTION: NOW EXTINCT as a result of the destruction of the native forest, and introduction of rats and cats. Occurred on Rodrigues and offshore islets. Probably extinct on the main island of Rodrigues by the 1870s. Last collected on one of the small, offshore islets in 1917. Rats are now established on all of the offshore islands and thorough searches in the 1960s and 1970s on all offshore islets have failed to yield any signs of this lizard.

TYPICAL HABITAT: The native forest before it was chopped and burned down for use as fuel and to make way for agricultural crops. Fed on insects, pollen, and fruit.

BRIEF DESCRIPTION: Several descriptive accounts of this species were made from the late 17th through the early 19th centuries. This was a thick-bodied robust diurnal lizard which was bright green, with a profusion of bright blue spots on the dorsal surface. The chin was deep yellow, and the underside of the tail light yellow. It was noted that this species, like most other *Phelsuma*, was capable of rapid color changes. This lizard was documented as not having a fear of humans and "was very tame, coming to eat fruits in one's hand." All that remains of this species today are six preserved specimens, three of which are in the British Museum, the three others in the Paris Museum.

Phelsuma flavigularis

SCIENTIFIC NAME: *Phelsuma flavigularis*

COMMON NAME: Yellow-throated day gecko

WHO DESCRIBED THE TAXON AND WHEN: Mertens, 1962.

TOTAL LENGTH: Averages 4.75-5.25 in. (12.1-13.3 cm). Males are larger than females.

DISTRIBUTION: Eastern Madagascar including the Perinet region. Difficult to find and appears to have very limited distribution.

TYPICAL HABITAT: Banana trees, small bushes, and on the ground.

BRIEF DESCRIPTION: Dorsally, light green with reddish markings on the head and small reddish spotting in the mid-dorsal area, with increased rust-colored spotting on the tail. Legs are grayish green and the throat is light yellow.

MANAGEMENT AND BREEDING IN CAPTIVITY: House singly or in sexual pairs in a well-planted vivarium. Only compatible individuals can be housed together. If skin rips are noted on the female, pull the male out immediately and house separately. Males of this species have a tendency to be too aggressive with the female during courtship in an enclosed area, so be sure to closely monitor male for aggression.

Yellow-throated day gecko *(Phelsuma flavigularis),* an uncommon Madagascar taxon. Photo by John Tashjian at Tim Tytle's breeding facility.

Phelsuma gigas

SCIENTIFIC NAME: *Phelsuma gigas*

COMMON NAME: Rodrigues giant day gecko

WHO DESCRIBED THE TAXON AND WHEN: Lienard, 1842.

TOTAL LENGTH: Approximately 2 ft (38 cm) or more, and thick bodied.

DISTRIBUTION: NOW EXTINCT as a result of the destruction of the native forest and introduction of rats and cats. Occurred on Rodrigues and offshore islets. Last collected in 1842 on the offshore islet of Ile aux Fregates.

TYPICAL HABITAT: Native forest, before it was destroyed by humans.

BRIEF DESCRIPTION: This was the largest species of day gecko *(Phelsuma)*. It was grayish or grayish brown with irregular black spotting. The tail was dark gray or charcoal-colored, with some striping. The tongue was pink in color. Ventrally, the lizard was light yellow. It was nocturnal in habit. The original type specimens have been lost and all that remains today are portions of several skeletons.

Phelsuma guentheri

SCIENTIFIC NAME: *Phelsuma guentheri*

COMMON NAME: Round Island day gecko

WHO DESCRIBED THE TAXON AND WHEN: Boulenger, 1885.

TOTAL LENGTH: Adult males average about 9.5 in. (24 cm) and females 9 in. (22.9 cm). Large individuals are capable of reaching almost 1 ft (30.5 cm).

DISTRIBUTION: Limited to the small, 375 acre, rat-free, dome-shaped islet of Round Island, 12.5 miles (20 km) NNE of Mauritius. Before massive habitat destruction by humans and the introduction of rats, cats, and other predators onto Mauritius, circa 1600, this lizard occurred on the main island of Mauritius as well. It is now restricted solely to Round Island. The habitat on Round Island was severely degraded by rabbits and goats released in the 1800s. These introduced mammals fortunately have now been eliminated.

TYPICAL HABITAT: Inhabits fan palms *(Lantania)*, pandanus, and bottle palms. Sometimes encountered in and around rocky crevices. Although it may be out during the day, recent studies have shown that it is most active at night. Courtship is primarily during the

Round Island day gecko *(Phelsuma guentheri)*. A CITES Appendix I species.
Photo by Nick Garbutt.

A Round Island day gecko *(Phelsuma guentheri)* communal egg-laying site under a rock overhang. Females consume the egg shell from hatched eggs to replenish their calcium reserves. Photo by Nick Garbutt.

A beautifully marked Round Island day gecko *(Phelsuma guentheri)*. These colors are not typically displayed by most individuals. Photo by Nick Garbutt.

summer. In the wild, females are colony nesters, selecting protected sites for egg deposition.

BRIEF DESCRIPTION: Adults are gray or brownish gray dorsally. Ventral surface is off-white. When basking, darker dorsal spots are present. A faint, dark-colored eye stripe is present from behind the nostril to above the ear opening. While generally somewhat plain in appearance, a few individuals in the wild have thin pale yellow barring on the toes and legs and very light mint green striping and barring on the dorsal surface, with off-white or light gray markings on the lips, throat, and flanks when in peak coloration. Juveniles of this species are typically light gray with a pattern of dark blotches and, in neonates and small juveniles, barring is present on the tail. The ventral surface is yellowish with dark brown barring.

MANAGEMENT AND BREEDING IN CAPTIVITY: This species is listed as endangered by the U.S. Department of the Interior (USDI) and as Appendix 1 by the Convention in the Trade in Endangered Species (CITES). It has been legally exported only by the Jersey Wildlife Preservation Trust Zoo in England. Thus, it has only been bred by Jersey WPT and a few private herpetoculturists in Holland and Germany, with specimens on loan from Jersey. Those at Jersey WPT are housed in glass vivaria measuring 39.5 x23.6 x 23.6 in. (100x60x60 cm). VitaLites® are used. The distance from lights to lizards is as little as 3 in. (8 cm). Plants are maintained in enclosures in pots, and newspaper is used as an substrate, for hygiene. Adult lizards are fed moths, including wax moth larvae and adults, butterflies, crickets, and grasshoppers, two times a week; once a week they are offered a fruit baby food mixed with vitamins and minerals. The lizards are housed both as sexual pairs and as individuals, introduced in January during the peak breeding period.

During courtship, the male arches his back, slowly flicking out his tongue and moving his body in a series of rapid jerky motions, following which copulation takes place. During laying cycles, egg clutches average 35 days apart. One to two eggs are laid. These are glued onto the sides of the tank and must be covered and incubated *in situ.* Incubation at Jersey WPT varies from 53-68 days. Females average one to four clutches a year. The young average 3 in. (7.5 cm) in total length and are reared in separate vivaria under Vita Lites®. For some reason not yet understood, the sex ratio of captive-bred offspring has been heavily skewed in favor of females.

Phelsuma guimbeaui

SCIENTIFIC NAME: *Phelsuma guimbeaui guimbeaui*

COMMON NAME: Mauritius lowland forest day gecko; orange-spotted day gecko

WHO DESCRIBED THE TAXON AND WHEN: Mertens, 1963.

TOTAL LENGTH: A mid-size species; males average 5-7 in. (12.7-17.8 cm), while females average 3.5- 5.1 in. (9-13 cm).

DISTRIBUTION: Mauritius, on the western side of the island at low and mid elevation.

TYPICAL HABITAT: Restricted to remnants of the native forest, narrow strips of trees along stream drainages and introduced coconut palms within its historic range.

BRIEF DESCRIPTION: Both males and females are thick-bodied, and males are significantly larger than females. One of the most strikingly colored of the day geckos. When at peak coloration, this lizard is brilliant green, with a diffuse light blue patch on the neck region. Bright orange barring is present on the head, and irregular-shaped brilliant orange spots and bars continue onto the body and tail. The body stripes are bordered by orange lines or dorso-lateral stripes. The tip of the tail may be blue. Ventrally, one or two light brown, v-shaped bars are present on the chin, and light brown spotting may be present on the throat. The entire ventral surface is typically a pale yellow. In the wild, lives in large colonies on huge forest trees. Rather shy, as heavily predated on by endemic and introduced birds. An "egg gluer," and frequently a colony nester. Eggs are often laid in tree hollows and neonates may be encountered under loose bark or between grooves in the bark.

MANAGEMENT AND BREEDING IN CAPTIVITY: Breeds best if housed in large, vertically oriented enclosures with live plants. Each enclosure may contain a single male and several adult females, all of similar size. Prefers daytime temperatures in the mid to high 80s°F (29-32°C), and nighttime temperatures in the high 60s to low 70s°F (19-22°C). Requires considerable experience with delicate *Phelsuma* species to successfully manage and breed. The eggs frequently need to be incubated *in situ.* Neonates are gray or charcoal, with light and dark dotting. Hatchlings vary in total length from 1.1-

1.5 in. (2.9-3.8 cm). They are extremely shy and require a number of hiding places in their rearing enclosure. During the first week, hatchlings often refuse insects but will lick sliced papaya or a baby food/nectar mixture. This supplementation is critical for their survival. The enclosure must also be heavily misted several times per day, as the small body size of these neonates allows for rapid desiccation. Up to four hatchlings of similar size may be reared together in a 6-10 gallon (23-38 liter) enclosure. Neonates do best if given mid-size branches with rough bark and live plants in their enclosures. Standard reptile tanks with sliding tops are not suitable as the neonates are capable of fitting into the top groove and may be crushed when the top is opened. Instead, house in a plastic terrarium with the opening at the center of the top directly under full-spectrum lighting. Proper care during the first several weeks is critical for their survival. Uncommon in captive collections.

A male Mauritius lowland forest day gecko *(Phelsuma g. guimbeaui)*. It is sometimes also called the orange-spotted day gecko. Photo by the author.

SCIENTIFIC NAME: *Phelsuma guimbeaui rosagularis*

COMMON NAME: Mauritius upland forest day gecko

WHO DESCRIBED THE TAXON AND WHEN: Vinson, 1969.

TOTAL LENGTH: Essentially, the same as *Phelsuma g. guimbeaui*.

DISTRIBUTION: Mauritius, upland forest, very little of which remains intact. Basks high on tree trunks, morning and late afternoon. Very dependent on suitable habitat. Populations are disjunct.

TYPICAL HABITAT: Large, endemic (native to Mauritius) forest trees. Does not typically utilize traveler's palms, bananas, or other secondary vegetation within or bordering patches of native forest.

BRIEF DESCRIPTION: The entire lizard is charcoal-colored when it first emerges from cavities in the tree, or from under tree bark, to bask in the early morning sun. The colors rapidly change to brilliant green with rust-colored spots, bars, and stripes, the arrangement of which is generally similar to *P. g. guimbeaui*. The rear portion of the tail may be blue. Chin is rust-colored, and typically without barring. Background color of the ventral surface is light gray. Charcoal-colored barring and spotting is often present on the ventral surface and in appearance resembles the surface of the tree bark on which the lizard lives. In some specimens, the dark ventral markings are reduced. At this high elevation, nights can be quite cool. Cavities in both tree trunks and large branches are important retreat sites. This is true not only at night, but also during cool or rainy weather, as well as during portions of the cyclone season.

MANAGEMENT AND BREEDING IN CAPTIVITY: Requires the same management as its lowland forest relative, *Phelsuma g. guimbeaui*. Extremely rare in captive collections.

Male Mauritius upland forest day gecko *(Phelsuma guimbeaui rosagularis).*
Photo by the author.

A juvenile Mauritius upland forest day gecko *(Phelsuma guimbeaui rosagularis)* **lacks the color-changing abilities it will possess later in life. Photo by the author.**

Phelsuma guttata

SCIENTIFIC NAME: *Phelsuma guttata*

COMMON NAME: None

WHO DESCRIBED THE TAXON AND WHEN: Kaudern, 1922.

TOTAL LENGTH: A mid-size species averaging about 5 in. (12.7 cm).

DISTRIBUTION: Eastern Madagascar, including the Fandrazana region, and along the coast, and in small areas of land between rivers.

TYPICAL HABITAT: No primary rainforest remains in the areas of eastern Madagascar where this species is typically found. It is encountered on bushes bordering rivers, on the ground, and on introduced banana trees.

BRIEF DESCRIPTION: A long-snouted light green lizard with a black eye stripe and charcoal or gray spotting and barring on the head, neck, flanks, legs, and tail. Several mid-size orange spots are prominent on the middle and lower portions of the back when in peak coloration. When less active, may be light bluish green with maroon-colored dots on the dorsal surface, and white speckling on the flank, legs, and feet. The ventral surface is mottled off-white and gray.

MANAGEMENT AND BREEDING IN CAPTIVITY: House and manage in a manner similar to *P. astriata*.

Phelsuma guttata, a mid-size species from Madagascar. Photo by R.D. Bartlett.

Phelsuma klemmeri, a tiny, recently-described species from Madagascar.
Photo by R.D. Bartlett.

Phelsuma klemmeri

SCIENTIFIC NAME: *Phelsuma klemmeri*

COMMON NAME: Yellow-headed day gecko

WHO DESCRIBED THE TAXON AND WHEN: Seipp, 1990.

TOTAL LENGTH: One of the smallest species of day gecko, only about 3.25-3.75 in. (8.3-9.5 cm).

DISTRIBUTION: Coastal northwest Madagascar

TYPICAL HABITAT: A rainforest species that lives on large trees and, if alarmed, will retreat into crevices in the bark.

BRIEF DESCRIPTION: The head and neck are iridescent yellow, with small black speckles. The upper and mid-back is bright turquoise blue. The lower back and uppermost portion of the tail is light brown. The bulk of the tail is turquoise blue. A large black spot is present behind the eye, followed by a broad black dorso-lateral stripe which extends the length of the body. The body is laterally flattened, considerably more so than any other known day gecko. Taxonomically, this lizard appears to be quite distinct from other *Phelsuma*.

MANAGEMENT AND BREEDING IN CAPTIVITY: Manage in a well-planted vivarium, including a number of closely placed bamboo sticks between the vegetation for perching sites. Bromeliads and orchids are well suited to this species. Daytime temperatures should be 80-82°F (27-28°C), with a nighttime low of 68°F (20°C). Mist, morning and evening. The diet should mainly consist of hatchling to one week old crickets. You may also feed them vestigial-winged fruit flies, wax moths, and small wax moth larvae. Despite their small size, they appear hardy. This species is not an "egg gluer." Eggs are somewhat oval in shape and hatch in 39-52 days when incubated at 80°F (27°C) plus or minus 4°F (2°C). Hatchlings are extremely small, averaging only 0.9-1.1 in. (22-29 mm). Neonates are paler in color than adults and require hatchling crickets and wingless fruit flies. As a supplement, sliced papaya or a banana baby food/nectar mix may be placed in a baby food jar lid so it does not dry out. Manage neonates in a manner similar to *P. g. guimbeaui*.

Yellow-headed day gecko *(Phelsuma klemmeri)*. Note the flattened body.
Photo by R.D. Bartlett.

Two yellow-headed day geckos *(Phelsuma klemmeri)*. Photo by R.D. Bartlett.

Phelsuma laticauda

SCIENTIFIC NAME: *Phelsuma laticauda laticauda*

COMMON NAME: Gold dust day gecko

WHO DESCRIBED THE TAXON AND WHEN: Boettger, 1880.

TOTAL LENGTH: 3.9-5.1 in (10-13 cm).

DISTRIBUTION: Madagascar, Comoros, introduced onto Farquhar Island in the southern Seychelles, and onto the Hawaiian islands, where it is established on both sides of Oahu, the Kona side of the Big Island, and on Maui.

TYPICAL HABITAT: Will utilize a variety of pantropic vegetation, including pandanus, coconut palms, bird of paradise, as well as human dwellings.

BRIEF DESCRIPTION: Background color is bright green to yellowish green. Light blue around the eyes. Three red finger markings on the back. Tail slightly flattened. Brilliant yellow speckles on the neck.

MANAGEMENT AND BREEDING IN CAPTIVITY: Prefers daytime temperatures of 82-89°F (28-32°C) with a 10-12°F (6-7°C) temperature drop at night. In addition to full-spectrum lighting, include a 50 or 75 watt sunspot lamp. Enclosure should have live plants plus vertical bamboo shoots for egg-laying. As with all day geckos, good air flow is important. Provide water through misting. Mist on a daily basis. Adults feed on first stage crickets, wax moth larvae, and flies. Dust the insect food with a vitamin/mineral powder and calcium carbonate. Females, as with other species of day geckos, store excess calcium for their eggs in chalk sacs at the side of their neck. In this species and several others, the females are ready to breed right after egg laying. Pairs should not be separated. Females lay one or, more often, two eggs, in a protected spot, such as a bamboo strip. As with other day geckos, immediately after laying, the eggs are held with the hind feet until their shells harden. Like most other Madagascar species, they are not "egg gluers." Eggs are laid in a protected location, such as at a plant leaf joint or inside a section of bamboo. Interestingly, with this species, if the eggs are not laid in a protected location, they are almost always infertile, and in such circumstances, may be eaten by the female. Eggs may be incubated at 82°F (28°C)

The gold dust day gecko *(Phelsuma l. laticauda).* A small, brightly colored species well suited for the hobbyist. Photo by Susan Schafer.

Phelsuma laticauda angularis, a colorful day gecko from northwest Madagascar. Photo by Ken T. Nemuras.

with high humidity. They will take 40-45 days to hatch at this temperature. The neonates are about 1.6 in. (4 cm) in length. The young can be raised singly or in pairs, in a small, planted vivarium. If a good nutritional balance is maintained, the lizards will be ready to breed within nine to twelve months. This species breeds well in captivity. Feed this species a diet of first stage crickets, wax moths, larvae and adults, flies, and a fruit supplement. Feed three times a week during most of the year, and twice a week during a standard two month 70-78°F (21-25°C) winter cool down.

SCIENTIFIC NAME: *Phelsuma laticauda angularis*

COMMON NAME: None

WHO DESCRIBED THE TAXON AND WHEN: Mertens, 1964.

TOTAL LENGTH: Averages 4-4.5 in. (10.2-11.4 cm).

DISTRIBUTION: Northwest Madagascar, including the region around Antsohihy.

TYPICAL HABITAT: Palms, pandanus, and other pantropic vegetation.

BRIEF DESCRIPTION: Smaller than the nominate form, with a flatter, wider tail, and less gold speckling. The number of femoral pores are reduced in males of this subspecies. Additionally, in place of the three large, red teardrop-shaped markings on the lower dorsal surface of the nominate form, there is a wide, irregular, inverted v-shaped marking.

MANAGEMENT AND BREEDING IN CAPTIVITY: Care instructions are the same as for *Phelsuma l. laticauda*.

Phelsuma leiogaster

SCIENTIFIC NAME: *Phelsuma leiogaster*

COMMON NAME: None

WHO DESCRIBED THE TAXON AND WHEN: Mertens, 1973.

TOTAL LENGTH: A small-size species. Males average 4.5 in. (3.8 cm) and females slightly over 3 in. (7.6 cm).

DISTRIBUTION: Southwest Madagascar, near the Tulear region, and south of Marambe. This area is extremely hot, with temperatures over 113°F (45°C) during the day and 86°F (30°C) at night.

TYPICAL HABITAT: On human dwellings, dead trees, and agave plants. Only active in the early morning and at night.

BRIEF DESCRIPTION: This is a light green lizard, with soft pastel shades. Males are olive green. Females are more of a grayish green. There are a series of light brown spots and bars present on the head, neck and back. A faint light gray lateral stripe separates the body from the white ventral surface. Feeds on mosquitoes and a variety of other small insects.

MANAGEMENT AND BREEDING IN CAPTIVITY: Management of this species is difficult. Males are considerably larger than females and can be very aggressive. There must be heavy planting and a number of hiding places in the enclosure. House individually, and introduce male for a several-day period at one-month intervals. If a particular male does not become too aggressive, maintain as a pair. Small agave and aloe are ideal enclosure plants for this species and for other *Phelsuma* from hot, dry areas of Madagascar.

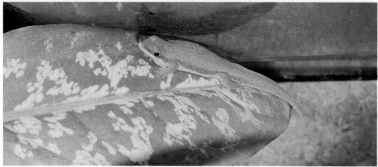

Phelsuma leiogaster, **originally described as a subspecies of** *P. lineata.* **Photo by Jurriaan Schulman.**

Phelsuma lineata

SCIENTIFIC NAME: *Phelsuma lineata lineata*

COMMON NAME: Lined day gecko

WHO DESCRIBED THE TAXON AND WHEN: Gray, 1842.

TOTAL LENGTH: Averages about 4.7 in. (12 cm).

DISTRIBUTION: The large island of Madagascar on the central plateau. It is common around the capital city of Antananarivo.

TYPICAL HABITAT: Pantropic vegetation (a variety of subtropical bushes and trees) and on human dwellings.

BRIEF DESCRIPTION: A small day gecko, males are typically an intense dark green, with many tiny red dots over most of the back. The green background color of the female is more subdued. A black lateral stripe separates the green dorsal surface from the whitish underside.

A female *Phelsuma lineata.* Photo by R.D. Bartlett.

SCIENTIFIC NAME: *Phelsuma lineata bombetokensis*

COMMON NAME: None

WHO DESCRIBED THE TAXON AND WHEN: Mertens, 1964.

TOTAL LENGTH: A small-size species reaching about 4 in. (10.2 cm).

DISTRIBUTION: Northwestern Madagascar including the region around Marovay.

TYPICAL HABITAT: The original habitat has essentially been destroyed, and what remains is savannah. This species lives on remaining palms, and on bushes by villages.

BRIEF DESCRIPTION: A thin, red stripe extends from the nostril to the eye. A faint, dusky dorso-lateral stripe extends from behind the eye to the tip of the tail. The dorsal surface is mottled light green or light brownish green. A faint, crescent-shaped marking is present on the back of the snout, with a faint bar behind the eyes. A series of large, irregular, light reddish blotches are present on the mid- and lower-back. A very distinctive, solid-colored, blackish purple oval is present on the side below the armpit area and a second similar oval-shaped marking is present on the uppermost portion of the rear leg.

MANAGEMENT AND BREEDING IN CAPTIVITY: House in a breeding group of one male with several females in a well-planted vivarium. Include medium-size bamboo strips, which will provide a suitable site for the female to lay her eggs.

SCIENTIFIC NAME: *Phelsuma lineata chloroscelis*

COMMON NAME: None

WHO DESCRIBED THE TAXON AND WHEN: Mertens, 1962.

TOTAL LENGTH: 4.9-5.75 in. (12.5-14.5 cm).

DISTRIBUTION: Central and east coast of Madagascar. Antanarivo to the region of Perinet. Introduced onto the island of Reunion in the early 1900s.

TYPICAL HABITAT: Lives on pantropic vegetation (bananas, palms, flowering bushes).

BRIEF DESCRIPTION: A large, irregular red spot which diffuses towards the back is present on a green background with a yellowish stripe between the dark side stripes and light-colored belly. The yellow dorso-lateral stripe is less developed in coastal specimens.

MANAGEMENT AND BREEDING IN CAPTIVITY: Well-planted vertical-format vivarium. The temperature should be 77-86°F (25-30°C) during the day with about a 10°F (6°C) drop at night. Specimens from the central plateau region of Madagascar need cool nighttime temperatures. Humidity during the day may be up to 75%. Males are larger than females. Females prefer clumps of vertically situated bamboo with a partially exposed, hollow top section for egg deposition. It is not uncommon for captive females to produce six sets of two eggs each during the year. To date, Europeans have had greater success routinely breeding this lizard than have Americans.

Phelsuma lineata chloroscelis. **This lizard is native to Madagascar and has been successfully introduced onto the island of Reunion. Photo by Dennis Sheridan.**

SCIENTIFIC NAME: *Phelsuma lineata dorsivittata*

COMMON NAME: None

WHO DESCRIBED THE TAXON AND WHEN: Mertens, 1964.

TOTAL LENGTH: 4-4.5 in. (10.2-11.4 cm).

DISTRIBUTION: Northern Madagascar, including the area around Joffreyville.

TYPICAL HABITAT: Area is quite moist with frequent rains at night which last for 4-5 hours. Lives on broadleaf trees in rocky areas.

BRIEF DESCRIPTION: A faint v-marking is present on the snout, extending to beyond the plane of the eyes. A short mid-dorsal stripe is present on the mid-body, followed by a series of irregular spots.

MANAGEMENT AND BREEDING IN CAPTIVITY: This is a rainforest species which has not yet been imported into the United States. It is rare in European collections. It has been successfully kept in a manner similar to *Phelsuma q. quadriocellata* and *Phelsuma lineata chloroscelis*.

SCIENTIFIC NAME: *Phelsuma lineata punctulata*

COMMON NAME: None

WHO DESCRIBED THE TAXON AND WHEN: Mertens, 1970.

TOTAL LENGTH: 4-5 in. (10.2 - 12.7 cm).

DISTRIBUTION: In the mountainous regions of northern Madagascar, including the region around Tsaratanana-Gebirge.

TYPICAL HABITAT: Traveler palms, other palms, and pantropic vegetation.

BRIEF DESCRIPTION: This taxon has a bright green dorsal surface, with a number of tiny red markings which extend from the middle of the back onto the tail. A typical *"lineata"* dorso-lateral white stripe is present. On the head, a red line is present from the nostril to the eye. A red triangle is typical between the eyes. The tail is a turquoise blue color.

MANAGEMENT AND BREEDING IN CAPTIVITY: Has not yet been imported into the United States.

Phelsuma madagascariensis

SCIENTIFIC NAME: *Phelsuma madagascariensis madagascariensis*

COMMON NAME: Madagascar day gecko

WHO DESCRIBED THE TAXON AND WHEN: Gray, 1831.

TOTAL LENGTH: Averages about 8.75 in. (22 cm).

DISTRIBUTION: Widely distributed in eastern Madagascar, and is found as well on the offshore islet of Ste. Marie. A population also occurs in the extreme southeast in the region around Fort Dauphin.

TYPICAL HABITAT: Inhabit trees along the edges of forests, pantropic vegetation, and human dwellings.

BRIEF DESCRIPTION: Green, light green, or greyish green, often with light skin color between the scales. A brownish-red eye stripe is typically present from the nostril to behind the eye. Small dots are sometimes present on top of the head. There may be brownish-red or red dots on the back. A thin, sometimes broken line may be present along the mid-back. Specimens from Ste. Marie are distinctive and typically have horizontal rows of white dots as juveniles.

MANAGEMENT AND BREEDING IN CAPTIVITY: House in a large, well-planted vivarium with many hiding places. If females are not ready to breed they can be damaged during courtship, as males tend to be aggressive. If a female does not have a chance to hide, she could be severely injured. House only compatible pairs together. Mist the entire enclosure well once daily. Vivarium temperatures should be maintained between 77-82°F (25-28°C). Mating and egg-laying typically occur between November and April. Large vertical bamboo stalks with partially open top sections are important for the females both to hide and lay eggs in. Typically, a female will lay one to two eggs up to six times a year. Eggs should be maintained at 82°F (28°C) with 75% humidity. Following this regime, the young will typically hatch in 50-55 days. Neonates average 2.25-2.3 inches (5.5-5.8 cm) in total length. Europeans typically raise neonates individually in small vivaria. If you attempt to raise the young in pairs, be certain there is no aggression.

A Madagascar day gecko *(Phelsuma m. madagascariensis)*. Photo by Jurriaan Schulman.

A female Madagascar day gecko *(Phelsuma m. madagascariensis)*.
Photo by Ken T. Nemuras.

A subadult *Phelsuma m. madagascariensis* from the islet of Ste. Marie, off the east coast of Madagascar. Photo by the author.

Wild-caught, recently imported *Phelsuma madagascariensis boehmi.* The damaged areas of skin will grow back if the lizard is properly maintained and not further stressed. Photo by R.D. Bartlett.

SCIENTIFIC NAME: *Phelsuma madagascariensis boehmei*

COMMON NAME: Boehme's giant day gecko

WHO DESCRIBED THE TAXON AND WHEN: Meier, 1982.

TOTAL LENGTH: Averages about 8.75 in. (22 cm).

DISTRIBUTION: Confined to the general region around Perenet and Ranomafana, in eastern Madagascar.

TYPICAL HABITAT: Commonly utilizes rainforest species of trees. It is often found high in the canopy.

BRIEF DESCRIPTION: Dorsal surface is bright green. There is a wide reddish-brown eye stripe, bars, and other markings on the head. Many bars and dots are present on the back. The area between the scales is dark.

MANAGEMENT AND BREEDING IN CAPTIVITY: Vivarium height is important. The vivarium should be at least 32 inches (81 cm) in height. Clumps of thick vertical bamboo between the planting works well. Between November and January, maintain at a temperature of 77-86°F (25-30°C) during the day. Between July and August, maintain a daytime temperature of 77°F (25°C) dropping it to 59°F (15°C) at night. These temperatures correspond with those in its rainforest environment. Maintain eggs at 82°F (28°C). The incubation period at this temperature is typically 48-55 days. At birth, the neonates average between 2.4-2.6 in. (6-6.5 cm). This relatively newly described subspecies is still uncommon in captive collections.

SCIENTIFIC NAME: *Phelsuma madagascariensis grandis*

COMMON NAME: Madagascar giant day gecko

WHO DESCRIBED THE TAXON AND WHEN: Gray, 1870.

TOTAL LENGTH: Large, males averaging up to 11 in. (28 cm). Females are smaller. Male specimens of 12 in. (30 cm) have been recorded.

DISTRIBUTION: Widely distributed in northern Madagascar, including several of the offshore islets.

TYPICAL HABITAT: Trees, palms, other pantropic vegetation, and human dwellings.

Male Madagascar giant day gecko *(Phelsuma madagascariensis grandis)*. Photo by John Tashjian at Chaffee Zoological Gardens of Fresno, California.

BRIEF DESCRIPTION: Males are larger than females and have well-developed femoral pores. This lizard is typically bright green, with a red eye stripe that extends from the nostril to the eye. Large red spots may be present on the back. However, the amount of red is quite variable, and the degree of red spotting depends entirely on the individual, rather than the geographic area from which it originates. A few of the most colorful specimens may have a little blue spotting, as well as wide red spots or bars.

MANAGEMENT AND BREEDING IN CAPTIVITY: The vivarium should be planted with sturdy species, such as snake plant *(Sansevieria),* which these lizards will readily use as resting, basking, and egg-laying sites. Horizontal bamboo strips are useful for basking. Additionally, vertical bamboo stalks at least 2 in. (5 cm) in diameter, and partially hollow at the top, are useful for the female to retreat into when laying her eggs. These are excellent display animals that can be housed singly. If you want to breed them, house a male and a female together throughout the year. Ideally, the female should be only slightly smaller than, or equal to, the size of the male as courtship can be aggressive. Generally, a female should not be used for breeding unless she is at least a year old. If a female does not show proper courtship behavior, she may be attacked by the male. Compatibility of specimens is essential. The male will grab the skin along the female's neck in his mouth while copulating. The pair, if compatible, should not be separated, as separation may lead to future aggression. A female in an egg-laying cycle typically lays one or two eggs every four to six weeks. The heaviest breeding and egg-laying occurs between November and May. When the female is ready to lay, she will enter a section of bamboo, often lying on her back, and lay her eggs. She will gently hold each egg with her rear feet until the shell has hardened. Eggs should be maintained at a temperature of 82°F (28°C) and 75% humidity. At this regime, the eggs will hatch in 47-65 days. The size of the neonates is significant, typically from 2.6-2.8 in. (6.7 - 7 cm) in length. With this taxon, it is best to raise each of the young separately in small vivaria.

Female Madagascar giant day gecko *(Phelsuma madagascariensis grandis)*. Note the well-developed chalk sacs. Photo by Ken T. Nemuras.

SCIENTIFIC NAME: *Phelsuma madagascariensis kochi*

COMMON NAME: Koch's giant day gecko

WHO DESCRIBED THE TAXON AND WHEN: Mertens, 1954.

TOTAL LENGTH: Large, 9-10 in. (22.9-25.4 cm) with exceptional specimens approaching 1 ft (30.5 cm).

DISTRIBUTION: Northwest and western Madagascar, on the coast and inland, including the Maevatanana region.

TYPICAL HABITAT: It occurs on banana trees, in banana plantations, and on other pantropic vegetation.

BRIEF DESCRIPTION: The v-shaped marking on the snout is greatly reduced. Faint reddish brown dots or dashes may be present at irregular intervals on the head. The sides of the neck and body are often light gray with brown mottling; the undersurface, off-white. Specimens imported into the United States and Europe during the 1970s and 1980s were typically a dull green with little, if any, bright-colored body spotting. However, this subspecies is quite variable in appearance throughout its natural range. Some populations have extensive red and/or orange spotting on the back, and are as attractive to the human eye as the most colorful *P. m. grandis*. As with other *P. madagascariensis,* males can be distinguished from females by their well-developed femoral pores.

MANAGEMENT AND CAPTIVE BREEDING: Easy to keep and breed. House in a manner similar to *Phelsuma m. grandis*. When incubated at 82°F (28°C) plus or minus 2°F (1°C), eggs typically hatch in 50-55 days.

Koch's day gecko *(Phelsuma madagascariensis kochi)*. Very hardy, variable amounts of red color. Photo by R.D. Bartlett.

Phelsuma minuthi

SCIENTIFIC NAME: *Phelsuma minuthi*

COMMON NAME: None

WHO DESCRIBED THE TAXON AND WHEN: Borner, 1980.

DISTRIBUTION: Madagascar, exact location unknown to author

Phelsuma modesta

SCIENTIFIC NAME: *Phelsuma modesta*

COMMON NAME: None

WHO DESCRIBED THE TAXON AND WHEN: Mertens, 1970.

TOTAL LENGTH: One of the smallest day geckos, averaging only 3 in. (7.6 cm).

DISTRIBUTION: Southern Madagascar, 20-50 miles (32-80 km) south of Ambovombe.

TYPICAL HABITAT: Dry, desert-like area, with endemic thorn forest and euphorbia-like plants.

BRIEF DESCRIPTION: This lizard is gray in color and, when at peak coloration, looks a little like a female *P. leiogaster.*

MANAGEMENT AND BREEDING IN CAPTIVITY: House in pairs and maintain in a well-planted vivarium, with agave and aloe vera. Keep their enclosure dry. Females show a tendency to become unusually stressed during egg laying. Therefore, remove the male when eggs are noticeable through the ventral surface of the female, and do not reintroduce until several weeks after egg laying. Rarely exported and rare in captive collections to date.

Phelsuma mutabilis

SCIENTIFIC NAME: *Phelsuma mutabilis*

COMMON NAME: None

WHO DESCRIBED THE TAXON AND WHEN: Grandidier, 1869.

TOTAL LENGTH: Both sexes are similar in size, 3-4 in. (7.6-10.2 cm).

DISTRIBUTION: Western Madagascar, including Menabe and Nosy Makamby.

TYPICAL HABITAT: Old acacia trees and stands of large bamboo. Typically found in holes in these trees. This is one of the hottest areas in Madagascar, with daytime temperatures that can climb to over 122°F (50°C).

BRIEF DESCRIPTION: Its coloring makes it "un-day gecko-like" in appearance. Bright colors of any kind are absent. Typically, this is a mottled gray lizard, with a black eye stripe that extends from the nostril to the back of the head. It can also be brownish gray with silver streaking. Juveniles are silver-colored. Active only in the early morning and at night. Feeds on insects.

MANAGEMENT AND BREEDING IN CAPTIVITY: A strong, hardy species. Keep hot and dry. Include snake plant *(Sansevieria)* and euphorbia. House in sexual pairs or one male with several females. Eggs take 65-67 days to hatch when incubated at 82°F (28°C), plus or minus 2°F (1°C). Typically breeds well in captivity, although uncommon in captive collections.

Phelsuma mutabilis, a drab colored, semi-arboreal species which, in the wild, often lives on or under rocks. Photo by R.D. Bartlett.

Phelsuma nigristriata, a small, rarely imported species from the Comoros. Photo by John Tashjian at Tim Tytle's breeding facility.

Phelsuma nigristriata

SCIENTIFIC NAME: *Phelsuma nigristriata*

COMMON NAME: None

WHO DESCRIBED THE TAXON AND WHEN: Meier, 1984.

TOTAL LENGTH: Averages 4.25 in. (10.8 cm).

DISTRIBUTION: Comoros, but with very limited distribution and range. Occurs in an area that is fairly moist.

TYPICAL HABITAT: Large clumps of old feral banana trees. Eggs are laid under joints of dried banana leaves.

BRIEF DESCRIPTION: A small, colorful day gecko with a black U-shaped mark on the nose, which continues as a line past the eye, along the flank, to the tail. Three faint gray stripes extend from the back of the head along the neck to the uppermost part of the body. These are bordered by light green or light turquoise stripes. A paired series of reddish spots are present on the mid and lower back. The tail has faint red barring. The dorsal surface is white.

MANAGEMENT AND BREEDING IN CAPTIVITY: As with other day gecko species, the author prefers using topsoil as substrate. Watering portions of the soil is very useful in keeping humidity levels within the desired range. For this species, include small potted yucca plants and snake plant *(Sansevieria)*. Also, include mid-size stalks of bamboo, as females will frequently lay their eggs in the hollow section. Bamboo stalks should be of an interior diameter that is slightly larger than the body width of the female, so that she can crawl into it easily to hide or to deposit eggs. The stalks should not have too great a width, i.e., mid-size width bamboo stalks would be used with mid-size species, such as this one.

Phelsuma ornata

SCIENTIFIC NAME: *Phelsuma ornata ornata*

COMMON NAME: Mauritius ornate day gecko

WHO DESCRIBED THE TAXON AND WHEN: Gray, 1825.

TOTAL LENGTH: 4-5 in. (10.2-12.7 cm). Not as sexually dimorphic (different) in size and color as other Mauritius *Phelsuma*. However, males are easily differentiated by their well-developed preanal pores.

DISTRIBUTION: Island of Mauritius, an area of about 969 sq. miles (2,512 sq km), and outlying islets, including Round Island.

TYPICAL HABITAT: Drier areas of Mauritius at low- and mid-elevation, and on a number of offshore islets. Utilizes a variety of trees and bushes, and may occasionally be found living on large rocks where the vegetation has been destroyed.

BRIEF DESCRIPTION: One of the most beautiful of all day geckos. A small-size, extremely colorful species. When in peak coloration, the head is bright red, a blue-green bar is present on the snout and another above each eye. The back of the head and neck are brown, bordered by white neck stripes. The body is bright blue, with rows of deep red spots. The tail is turquoise blue, with reddish or rust-colored bars. The legs and lower flanks are grayish. The ventral surface is off-white. In the wild, feeds on nectar from flowers, pollen from palms, and insects. Eggs are laid in individual clutches in leaf joints, or communally, under protected rocky surfaces or tree bark.

MANAGEMENT AND BREEDING IN CAPTIVITY: House in pairs and manage in a manner similar to *P. laticauda*.

SCIENTIFIC NAME: *Phelsuma ornata inexpectata*

COMMON NAME: Reunion Island ornate day gecko

WHO DESCRIBED THE TAXON AND WHEN: Mertens, 1966.

TOTAL LENGTH: 4-4.5 in. (10.2-11.4 cm).

DISTRIBUTION: Coastal areas of Reunion Island, in the region of Manapany-les-Bains.

A Mauritius island ornate day gecko *(Phelsuma o. ornata)*. A versatile species that prefers drier habitats. It is only rarely imported into the United States. Photo by the author.

A male Reunion Island ornate day gecko *(Phelsuma ornata inexpectata)*. These are very delicate and rare in captivity. Photo by the author.

TYPICAL HABITAT: Inhabits pandanus, banana, papaya, other pantropic vegetation, and human dwellings. Habitat is relatively hot and dry.

BRIEF DESCRIPTION: Reddish markings are present on the snout and front of the eyes. The upper part of the snout is dark blue. A wide brown stripe extends from behind the eye to the shoulder. The back and tail are iridescent green with a network of small reddish lines and dots. The reddish body spotting is greatly reduced in females.

MANAGEMENT AND BREEDING IN CAPTIVITY: House in a vertically-oriented enclosure with live plants, such as *Dracaena marginata.* This taxon may be managed either in pairs or as a colony species, with a male and several females. Prefers daytime temperatures in the mid to high 80s°F(29-32°C), and nighttime temperatures in the low 70s°F (21-23°C). Neonates are surprisingly large and average 1.9 in. (48 mm) in total length. The egg incubation period is 50-52 days when incubated at 82°F (28°C), plus or minus 2°F (1°C). Very rare in captive collections in the United States, and uncommon in European collections.

A female Reunion island ornate day gecko *(Phelsuma ornata inexpectata).*
Photo by the author.

Phelsuma parkeri

SCIENTIFIC NAME: *Phelsuma parkeri*

COMMON NAME: Pemba Island day gecko

WHO DESCRIBED THE TAXON AND WHEN: Loveridge, 1941.

TOTAL LENGTH: A small-size species.

DISTRIBUTION: Pemba Island, Tanzania.

TYPICAL HABITAT: Coastal lowland, pantropic vegetation.

BRIEF DESCRIPTION: Extremely similar in appearance to *Phelsuma dubia.*

MANAGEMENT AND BREEDING IN CAPTIVITY: Manage in a manner similar to *P. dubia.*

Phelsuma pusilla

SCIENTIFIC NAME: *Phelsuma pusilla pusilla*

COMMON NAME: None

WHO DESCRIBED THE TAXON AND WHEN: Mertens, 1964.

TOTAL LENGTH: One of the smallest day gecko species. This taxon reaches only 2.5-3.25 in. (6.4-8.3 cm).

DISTRIBUTION: Eastern Madagascar, including the Ambila - Lemaitso region, and on the offshore islet of Ste. Marie.

TYPICAL HABITAT: Is found in a relatively moist area on the east coast, where it is common for short rainstorms to occur each day. Lives on small trees and euphorbia-like plants.

BRIEF DESCRIPTION: The dorsal surface is lime green. There are two red bars on the head and two rows of broken red lines extend from the mid back to the tail. A black lateral line extends from behind the nostril to the rear legs. The ventral surface is white.

MANAGEMENT AND BREEDING IN CAPTIVITY: This species requires specialized management. House singly in a very well-planted ten gallon (38 liter) size vivarium with multiple hide areas. Put the male in with the female to breed. Remove the male to his own enclosure when the eggs are visible through the ventral surface of the female. Return male to the female's enclosure one month after she has laid. The reason for this is that males of this taxon are too aggressive in their courtship attempts with the female. In a captive situation, there is not enough space for the female to move away from the male's advances.

SCIENTIFIC NAME: *Phelsuma pusilla hallmanni*

COMMON NAME: Hallmann's day gecko

WHO DESCRIBED THE TAXON AND WHEN: Meier, 1989

TOTAL LENGTH: A very small species, only growing to 3.1-3.5 in. (79-89 mm).

DISTRIBUTION: Eastern Madagascar, including the region around Perinet.

TYPICAL HABITAT: Found in habitat which also supports *P. q. quadriocellata,* including bushes, traveler palms, and on banana trees.

BRIEF DESCRIPTION: A small, brightly-colored, sexually dimorphic species. One of the most beautifully marked of any of the day geckos. When this taxon is in active (peak) coloration, a turquoise blue triangle is present on the snout, bordered from behind by a red bar. The back of the head and neck have bluish green speckles. The back is bright lime green, with a series of more or less parallel, irregular reddish blotches. A black lateral stripe extends from the armpit to the front of the rear legs. The tail is turquoise. The legs and feet are speckled with beige and light green.

A four spot or peacock day gecko *(Phelsuma q. quadriocellata).* A small, colorful species from Madagascar. Photo by the author.

Phelsuma quadriocellata

SCIENTIFIC NAME: *Phelsuma quadriocellata quadriocellata*

COMMON NAME: Four spot or peacock day gecko

WHO DESCRIBED THE TAXON AND WHEN: Peters, 1883.

TOTAL LENGTH: Averages about 4.7 in. (12 cm).

DISTRIBUTION: Eastern Madagascar, including the region around Perinet.

TYPICAL HABITAT: Pantropic vegetation, including banana plants, and human dwellings.

BRIEF DESCRIPTION: Forest green back with red dots and stripes. A blue v-shaped marking may be present on the snout, and tiny blue speckles may be present on the neck. A large, black or navy blue spot, outlined in turquoise, is present in the armpit area behind the front legs with another dark area in front of the rear limbs.

MANAGEMENT AND BREEDING IN CAPTIVITY: House in a well planted vertical format vivarium. Include vertical bamboo stalks, each having a diameter of 0.75 in. (2 cm). Be sure that the top segments are partially open, so that the female can enter to lay eggs. Maintain these lizards at 82-86°F (28-30°C), with a nighttime drop in temperature to 68°F (20°C). This species likes high humidity. Daytime humidity levels of 75% are desired, with a heavy misting in the evening. This species breeds best if temperatures are dropped to 75°F (24°C) during the day, and 60-65°F (16-18°C) at night during the months of July and August. Only a single pair should be housed together. If the female is in an egg-laying cycle, she will typically lay two eggs every 3-5 weeks, averaging about six sets of eggs a year. Usually, the eggs are deposited in the hollow vertical bamboo, but on occasion they will be attached to leaves. The eggs should be incubated at a temperature of 82°F (28°C), with about 75% humidity. Following this regime, the eggs will take 40-45 days to hatch. The neonates average 1.2 in. (3 cm) in length and will take pinhead crickets, wingless fruit flies, and a fruit supplement.

SCIENTIFIC NAME: *Phelsuma quadriocellata leiura*

COMMON NAME: None

WHO DESCRIBED THE TAXON AND WHEN: Meier, 1983.

TOTAL LENGTH: A small-size species.

DISTRIBUTION: Southeast Madagascar, including the area around Imotra.

TYPICAL HABITAT: Trees and bushes.

BRIEF DESCRIPTION: A very colorful taxon which is green or greenish purple with a metallic sheen.

MANAGEMENT AND BREEDING IN CAPTIVITY: Extremely uncommon in captivity. As yet, has not been imported into the United States. May be housed in breeding groups of a single male and up to 3 females in a well-planted vivarium.

SCIENTIFIC NAME: *Phelsuma quadriocellata parva*

COMMON NAME: None

WHO DESCRIBED THE TAXON AND WHEN: Meier, 1981.

TOTAL LENGTH: Males average 3.5-4 in. (8.9-10.2 cm) and females 3-3.5 in. (7.6-8.9 cm).

DISTRIBUTION: Eastern Madagascar, including the region around Tamatave.

TYPICAL HABITAT: Secondary forest and bushes in areas away from human habitation.

BRIEF DESCRIPTION: Extremely colorful with very bright green, blues, and purple, with a metallic sheen.

MANAGEMENT AND BREEDING IN CAPTIVITY: Manage in groups of one male with two or three females in a well-planted enclosure. Extremely uncommon in captivity and, as yet, has not been bred routinely.

Phelsuma robertmertensi

SCIENTIFIC NAME: *Phelsuma robertmertensi*

COMMON NAME: Robert Merten's day gecko

WHO DESCRIBED THE TAXON AND WHEN: Meier, 1980.

TOTAL LENGTH: An average length of 4.25-4.5 in. (10.8-11.4 cm). Neonates average 1.4 in. (3.5 cm).

DISTRIBUTION: Comoros.

TYPICAL HABITAT: Old, wild banana trees and abandoned vanilla orchid plantations.

BRIEF DESCRIPTION: A small attractively marked day gecko. Can be somewhat variable in color and the species is also sexually dichromatic. When in peak coloration, has a wide turquoise blue bar on the snout, with similar color above the eyes, and turquoise blue extending down the middle of the back onto the tail. Inside this band of turquoise on the back is a broken mid-dorsal orange stripe. The sides of the neck, flanks and legs are light brown. When somewhat less active, this lizard is a light turquoise blue with a broken, rust brown mid-dorsal stripe. The female is essentially a chocolate brown lizard with a light blue bar on the nose, a light blue ring around the eye, a faint thin rust-colored mid-dorsal stripe, bordered by chocolate brown with diffuse mint green spotting extending dorso-laterally from the neck, down the body, onto the upper tail.

MANAGEMENT AND BREEDING IN CAPTIVITY: Manage as you would *P. nigristriata.* Eggs 49-52 days to hatch when incubated at 82°F (28°C), plus or minus 2°F (1°C).

Robert Merten's day gecko *(Phelsuma robertmertensi)*, a small species from the Comoros. Photo by the author.

Seipp's day gecko *(Phelsuma seippi)*, a recently-described species from Madagascar. Photo by R.D. Bartlett.

Phelsuma seippi

SCIENTIFIC NAME: *Phelsuma seippi*

COMMON NAME: Seipp's day gecko

WHO DESCRIBED THE TAXON AND WHEN: Meier, 1987.

TOTAL LENGTH: A mid-size species averaging about 5-5.5 in. (12.7-14.0 cm).

DISTRIBUTION: Northern Madagascar, including the offshore island of Nosy Be.

TYPICAL HABITAT: This species is restricted to the native forest and may be found in trees both in the forest and along its edges.

BRIEF DESCRIPTION: The snout is rather pointed. A dark brown eye stripe extends from the back of the mouth to beyond the eye. The dorsal surface is green or light green with several reddish brown or maroon dots. Some specimens also have dorsal striping. The throat area is very distinct; it is light-colored with several dark, v-shaped markings.

MANAGEMENT AND BREEDING IN CAPTIVITY: This is a rainforest species and requires a well-planted vivarium. Select plants with smooth branches and mist frequently. It is not uncommon for this species to lay its eggs on the ground, under bark or fallen leaves. The eggs should be removed and incubated at 82°F (28°C). The neonates take between 48-50 days to hatch and are about 1.5-1.6 in. (3.8-4.0 cm) when they come out of the egg. Feed pinhead crickets and vestigial wing *Drosophila,* as well as a fruit supplement. Typically breeds well in captivity.

Seipp's day gecko *(Phelsuma seippi)hatchling.* **Photo by Tim Tytle.**

Phelsuma serraticauda

SCIENTIFIC NAME: *Phelsuma serraticauda*

COMMON NAME: Flat-tailed day gecko

WHO DESCRIBED THE TAXON AND WHEN: Mertens, 1963.

TOTAL LENGTH: Males average about 5 in. (13 cm), females are slightly smaller. Exceptional specimens can reach 6 in. (15.2 cm).

DISTRIBUTION: Eastern Madagascar, north of Tamatave.

TYPICAL HABITAT: Largely restricted to coconut palms *(Cocos nucifera)*. Present on coconut plantations within natural range. Therefore, would be an ideal species to commercially field-culture.

BRIEF DESCRIPTION: Dorsal background color is green or yellowish green. Three tear-shaped, prominent red markings are present on the back, before the tail. Has a distinctive broad, flattened tail with tiny serrated edges. The tail is broadest in males. In appearance, it is somewhat similar to *P. laticauda*, except for the flattened tail.

MANAGEMENT AND BREEDING IN CAPTIVITY: Feed these animals third stage crickets, flies, and wax moth larvae. In nature, these lizards live in colonies of a single male and several females, usually high up in the vegetation. Thus, they need to be maintained in captivity in large, vertically-oriented, well-planted enclosures. Most wild-caught individuals of this species are heavily parasitized and need to be wormed. An appropriate dosage of a standard wormer injected into a food item or sprinkled onto a fruit supplement will work effectively. The females have a well-developed dominance hierarchy, and each requires a specific territory. Females typically lay four sets of eggs, usually between December and March. If incubated at 82°F (28°C) with about 75% humidity, the eggs will take 53-58 days to hatch. Clutch mates often hatch one day apart. They are typically about 1.6 in. (4 cm) in length. European breeders prefer to raise the young in separate containers. Neonates will take pinhead crickets and vestigial-wing fruit flies.

A male flat-tailed day gecko *(Phelsuma serraticauda)*. A species with limited distribution in the wild. Photo by R.D. Bartlett.

Ventral view of a flat-tailed day gecko *(Phelsuma serraticauda)* clearly showing the broad, flat caudal appendage. Photo by R.D. Bartlett.

Phelsuma standingi

SCIENTIFIC NAME: *Phelsuma standingi*

COMMON NAME: Standing's day gecko

WHO DESCRIBED THE TAXON AND WHEN: Methuen and Hewitt, 1913.

TOTAL LENGTH: A large-size, thick-bodied day gecko. Males can be distinguished from females by their large, well-developed, brown colored femoral pores. Otherwise, males and females are similar in size and appearance and average 8.25-10 in. (21.0-25.4 cm), with exceptional specimens exceeding 11 in. (27.9 cm).

DISTRIBUTION: Southwest Madagascar, including the region around Andranolaho.

TYPICAL HABITAT: This species inhabits the dry southwest portion of Madagascar with its unique thorn forest vegetation. Until recently, this was one of the very few areas in Madagascar which was relatively undisturbed. However, charcoal burners are making inroads into its habitat, and for this reason *P. standingi* is now a species of special concern to the world's conservation organizations.

BRIEF DESCRIPTION: Hatchlings have a yellowish green head with a series of lines and bars. The neck and back are brown with a large number of thin, light-colored bands and bars extending the length of the back. These bands and bars become wider and more mint green-colored on the tail. This species looks quite different as an adult. Typically an adult is light gray with some light turquoise color on the head and tail, and tiny gray reticulated markings on the head and body. An exceptionally marked adult is light turquoise with small gray reticulations on the head and back and light gray flanks and upper legs.

MANAGEMENT AND BREEDING IN CAPTIVITY: The enclosure should be reasonably large with a vertical format. Several sturdy, live potted plants, such as snake plant *(Sansevieria),* are required. This species does well and breeds readily in captivity. No more than one pair should be housed together. Eggs are typically laid in plant leaf joints or under surface litter on the ground. When incubated at 82-84°F (28-29°C), eggs hatch in approximately 70

Standing's day gecko *(Phelsuma standingi).* A species from southern Madagascar that breeds well in captivity. Photo by Ken T. Nemuras.

A neonate Standing's day gecko *(Phelsuma standingi).* Photo by R.D. Bartlett.

days. One of the keys to breeding this species is to afford a temperature drop at night. Daytime temperatures should be in the mid 80s°F (29-30°C) with a small sun spot lamp affording a basking spot in the mid 90s°F (35°C). Nighttime temperatures should be dropped to 72-74°F (22-23°C). This species may become quite accustomed to humans and will typically accept dusted crickets and other insects from a person's fingers once it is well-acclimated.

A juvenile Standing's day gecko *(Phelsuma standingi).* **Photo by Ken T. Nemuras.**

Phelsuma s. sundbergi

SCIENTIFIC NAME: *Phelsuma sundbergi sundbergi*

COMMON NAME: Seychelles Giant day gecko

WHO DESCRIBED THE TAXON AND WHEN: Rendahl, 1939.

TOTAL LENGTH: Adult males may reach a maximum snout-vent length of 3.7 in. (95 mm) and a maximum total length of close to 10 in. (25.4 cm). Large adult females are only slightly smaller.

DISTRIBUTION: Praslin, Curieuse, and several other smaller islands in the northeast granitic Seychelles.

TYPICAL HABITAT: Lives on the huge coco-de-mer palms *(Lodoicea maldivica),* of the islands of Praslin and Curieuse. These lizards aid in the pollination of these palms by transferring pollen between male and female trees while feeding. Also, commonly found on coconut palms and other large trees, including sea grape, and occasionally on human dwellings. With this taxon, habitat choice is opportunistic and the size of the trees appears more important than the specific species of tree.

BRIEF DESCRIPTION: A large, bright green lizard sometimes with tiny rust-colored reticulated markings on the body and tail. A faint, rust-colored stripe is present on the side of the head from nostril to eye. Some barring is also present on the top of the snout. This may be the most difficult day gecko to sex correctly because males and females are similar in size and general appearance. Females also have slightly enlarged femoral pores. They can, however, be reliably sexed when in peak activity colors, as the femoral region is reddish brown in males. In the wild, a major part of the diet is pollen obtained from palm inflorescences. There is considerable resource partitioning between this species and *Phelsuma astriata,* which shares its general habitat. The considerably smaller *P. astriata* is eaten or aggressively pursued if it attempts to reside on larger trees inhabited by the former. Additionally, to minimize intraspecies aggression, juvenile *P. sundbergi* typically reside on the outer branches and fronds of the large trees. Females are colony nesters, sometimes utilizing holes in the trunks of palms to lay their eggs.

The incomparable Vallée de Mai on the island of Praslin, Seychelles. This is ideal habitat for *Phelsuma s. sundbergi* and *Ailuronyx seychellensis*. Photo by the author.

A close-up of the head of a Seychelles giant day gecko *(Phelsuma s. sundbergi)*, a species adapted to the coco-de-mer forests of Praslin and Curieuse. Photo by Ken T. Nemuras.

MANAGEMENT AND BREEDING IN CAPTIVITY: Manage in pairs in a manner similar to Madagascar giant day geckos. The eggs typically take 56-71 days to hatch when incubated at 82-84°F (28-29 C) plus or minus 2°F (1°C). Neonates are grayish green with a rust brown, irregular-shaped marking on top of the head and many small white dots are present on the body, legs, and upper surface of the feet. Neonates also have thin rows of small white spots along the dorsal surface of the tail. As is typical with most day gecko species, the outer layer of skin is shed and eaten within a short period of time after the lizard hatches.

SCIENTIFIC NAME: *Phelsuma sundbergi ladiguensis*

COMMON NAME: La Digue day gecko

WHO DESCRIBED THE TAXON AND WHEN: Bohme, 1980.

TOTAL LENGTH: Reaches a maximum snout-vent length of 3.25 in. (80 mm) and a total length of 7.5-8 in. (19.1-20.3 cm).

DISTRIBUTION: On the islands of La Digue and Marianne in the granitic Seychelles.

TYPICAL HABITAT: This lizard lives on coconut palm trees and surrounding vegetation.

BRIEF DESCRIPTION: Adults are generally similar to, but smaller in size than, *P. s. sundbergi,* from Praslin and Curieuse. Additionally, rust-colored dorsal markings on the adults are more pronounced. Dorsally green when active, charcoal-colored when inactive, with small rust-colored bars or dots. Neonates and juveniles of this subspecies are greenish with small rust colored bars on the back. Neonates and juveniles also have a thin, rust-colored, mid-dorsal stripe which begins over the plane of the front limbs. This stripe is typically absent in adults.

MANAGEMENT AND BREEDING IN CAPTIVITY: Manage in a manner similar to *P. s. sundbergi.*

Phelsuma s. sundbergi, a large taxon that usually adapts well in captivity.
Photo by the author.

La Digue day gecko *(Phelsuma sundbergi ladiguensis)* **from the Seychelles.**
Photo by the author.

SCIENTIFIC NAME: *Phelsuma sundbergi longisulae*

Prior to work on this taxon by Gardner in the 1980s, this taxon was sometimes classified as *Phelsuma longisulae pulchra.*

COMMON NAME: Mahé day gecko

WHO DESCRIBED THE TAXON AND WHEN: Rendahl, 1939.

TOTAL LENGTH: Maximum snout-vent length 2.7 in. (68 mm) and a total length of 6 in. (15.2 cm), although most adults in the wild have regenerated tails and are slightly smaller.

DISTRIBUTION: The western granitic islands of the Seychelles, including the large island of Mahé.

TYPICAL HABITAT: A mid-size species found in the greatest numbers at lower elevations. Well adapted to coconut plantations, gardens, trees, and bushes in association with human dwellings. Palms, including coconut palms, pandanus, plumeria, banana, and a variety of garden and backyard tropical trees, shrubs, and flowering plants. Lives sympatrically (in association) with *P.a. astriata.* Perhaps as a result of being similar in size, there is only partial resource partitioning, and both taxa may sometimes be found on the same tree or large bush. The average daytime temperature on Mahé is 86°F (30°C). The humidity range is 79-83%, and the rainfall on Mahé averages 91 in. (231 cm) per year. This is typical of lower elevation, mid- and small-size islands throughout the Indian Ocean. This information needs to be taken into account for the successful maintenance of most species of day geckos.

BRIEF DESCRIPTION: The snout is long with an irregular v-shaped marking from mid-snout to the rear of the head. Scales bordering the eyes are bright yellow. Dorsally, this lizard is blue-green. A series of rust-colored spots, dots, dashes, and bars extend the length of the lizard. The ventral surface is off-white. Occasionally, maroon or rust-colored spots are present at irregular locations.

MANAGEMENT AND BREEDING IN CAPTIVITY: House in pairs in well-planted vivaria .

Seychelles day geckos *(Phelsuma sundbergi longisulae)*. This was formerly called *Phelsuma longisulae pulchra*. Photographed on the island of Mahé by the author.

A juvenile *Phelsuma sundbergi longisulae.* Photo by the author.

Phelsuma trilineata

SCIENTIFIC NAME: *Phelsuma trilineata*

COMMON NAME: Three lined day gecko

WHO DESCRIBED THE TAXON AND WHEN: Gray, 1842.

Known only from a single type specimen.

A completed indoor enclosure. Note the wood feeding stations with papaya. Two sets of 4 ft shop light fixtures equipped with full-spectrum lighting rest on the top directly over horizontal basking strips. *Dracaena fragrans* are useful enclosure plants, serving as both watering and egg-laying stations. The enclosure, on rollers, can be moved outdoors when the weather is suitable. Photo by the author.

Phelsuma v-nigra

SCIENTIFIC NAME: *Phelsuma v-nigra v-nigra*

COMMON NAME: None

WHO DESCRIBED THE TAXON AND WHEN: Boettger, 1913.

TOTAL LENGTH: Males average 3.5-4 in. (8.9-10.2 cm) and females 3.5 in. (8.9 cm).

DISTRIBUTION: Found only on Moheli Island in the Comoros.

TYPICAL HABITAT: Large, feral banana trees and in villages, on dwellings and associated vegetation.

BRIEF DESCRIPTION: When in peak coloration, this lizard is a bright light green with a brilliant, diffuse, light bluish hue mid-dorsally and the entire length of the tail. Two rust-colored bars are present on the snout and a thin, broken mid-dorsal stripe extends from the middle of the head to the middle of the back. Many small rust-colored irregular dots are present on the back. The ventral surface of the lizard is lemon yellow.

MANAGEMENT AND BREEDING IN CAPTIVITY: House male and female separately in planted vivaria. Males should be kept individually. Females can be kept individually or in small groups. Introduce male into female's enclosure for several days on a monthly basis. Females typically go 3-4 months between periods of laying. Eggs typically take 58-60 days when incubated at 82°F (28°C) plus or minus 2°F (1°C). This taxon has only rarely been imported into the United States to date.

SCIENTIFIC NAME: *Phelsuma v-nigra anjouanensis*

COMMON NAME: Anjouan Island day gecko

WHO DESCRIBED THE TAXON AND WHEN: Meier, 1986.

TOTAL LENGTH: Males are 4-4.4 inches (10.2-11.4 cm). Females are slightly smaller.

DISTRIBUTION: Occurs only on Anjouan Island in the Comoros.

TYPICAL HABITAT: This species occurs in high densities in the wild, and utilizes a variety of habitats, including coconut palms, banana trees, agave bushes, dwellings, and is even found on the ground along the shoreline.

BRIEF DESCRIPTION: A light green lizard with light rust-colored barring on the nose, spotting on the top of the head, and many tiny rust-colored spots and reticulations extending on the back and tail. Ventrally, grayish white with a single, very faint chin stripe.

MANAGEMENT AND BREEDING IN CAPTIVITY: House in well-planted vivaria in pairs. Euphorbias, wax plants, and small agaves are suitable. Also include strips of medium-size bamboo. A female will lay her eggs inside a hollow section of bamboo. Soil is the preferred substrate. Mist enclosure twice daily but do not overwater substrate as this taxon prefers a slightly drier environment.

SCIENTIFIC NAME: *Phelsuma v-nigra comoraegrandensis*

COMMON NAME: Grand Comoro day gecko

WHO DESCRIBED THE TAXON AND WHEN: Meier, 1986.

TOTAL LENGTH: Both sexes average 3-4 in. (7.6-10.2 cm).

DISTRIBUTION: Limited distribution in the northern part of Grand Comoro Island (Comoros).

TYPICAL HABITAT: This is a rainforest species, occurring in moist forest and, where that no longer exists, on secondary vegetation. It may even be encountered on the ground.

BRIEF DESCRIPTION: Least colorful of any of the *P. v-nigra* subspecies. Dorsally, bluish green with a thin, broken, mid-dorsal stripe that extends from the head to the lower back. Light brown barring is present on the head and many irregular small light brown spots are present on the back and tail. Ventrally, a broad stripe is present on the lower portion of the chin. Light reticulated markings occur on the throat and lower flanks. The ventral surface of the body is light gray with a bluish tinge. The undersurface of the tail is light yellow with faint dark mottling.

MANAGEMENT AND BREEDING IN CAPTIVITY: Manage with soil as substrate and potted plants, such as snake plant *(Sansevieria)* and euphorbias. Include strips of bamboo for egg-laying. Keep relatively high humidity levels in the enclosure.

Phelsuma v-nigra from Grand Comoro Island. Photo by Eddy Postma.

Pasteur's day gecko *(Phelsuma v-nigra pasteuri)*, a small colorful taxon from the Comoros. Photo by the author.

SCIENTIFIC NAME: *Phelsuma v-nigra pasteuri*

COMMON NAME: Pasteur's day gecko

WHO DESCRIBED THE TAXON AND WHEN: Meier, 1984.

TOTAL LENGTH: A small-size taxon. Females average 3.5-4 in. (8.9-10.2 cm), males 4-4.5 in. (10.2-11.4 cm) with exceptional specimens reaching 5 in. (12.7 cm).

DISTRIBUTION: Moheli Island in the Comoros.

TYPICAL HABITAT: Banana trees and coconut palms.

BRIEF DESCRIPTION: An attractive, small-size species. Bright green with a reddish bar on the nose and another between the eyes and a thin ring of yellow around the eye. A diffuse turquoise blue patch is present on the neck. A thin, mid-dorsal stripe is often seen on the neck and uppermost part of the back, with a random series of reddish spots extending from mid-body to the upper portion of the tail.

MANAGEMENT AND BREEDING IN CAPTIVITY: House in pairs in a well-planted vivarium. Daytime temperatures should be in the mid 80s°F (29-30°C) and nighttime lows in the high 70s°F (24-26°C). Include a 2 month winter cooldown with daytime temperatures of 77-79°F (25-26°C) and nighttime drops to 63°F (17°C). During the simulated winter period, feed twice a week rather than every other day.

Ailuronyx seychellensis

SCIENTIFIC NAME: *Ailuronyx seychellensis*
A large gecko from the Seychelles which is NOT a day gecko but which requires much of the same type of care.

COMMON NAME:

English: Seychelles giant skin-sloughing gecko

German: Bronze gecko

WHO DESCRIBED THE TAXON AND WHEN: Dumeril and Bibron, 1836. Two additional taxa from the Seychelles are in the process of being described. Two of the three forms live sympatrically on the giant coco de mer palms on Praslin.

TOTAL LENGTH: The large form living on Praslin and Cousin averages 8-9 in. (20.3-22.9 cm), with exceptional specimens up to 10 in. (25 cm).

DISTRIBUTION: The granitic islands of the Seychelles.

TYPICAL HABITAT: Large palms, mature banana trees, walls and ceiling of human dwellings.

BRIEF DESCRIPTION: A large, "day gecko-like" arboreal lizard. Beautiful, with subtle yellow, light brown, dark brown colors. Skin rips **extremely** easily. Sloughing (ripping) of large pieces of skin is a defense mechanism against the small, endemic, feather-legged owl, which is its principal predator. These lizards are most active at night during which time they sometimes descend to the ground to take insect prey or to lick fallen fruit. During the day, they are usually visible in the crowns of palms or on the inner walls of dwellings, but are somewhat less active than at night. Typically, they have little fear of people and can be approached quite closely.

MANAGEMENT AND BREEDING IN CAPTIVITY: House in pairs in large, vertical-format vivaria. Adults will eat a variety of insects and lap nectar and lick fruit. A female will guard her eggs against others of her species. Typically, the eggs are laid in the open at an elevated location. They stick to the surface they are laid on and cannot be removed without damaging or breaking them. The eggs must be covered with a firm, clear plastic container to which small airholes have been added to allow for ventilation. A small section of paper towel should be placed in the bottom of the protective plastic cover. Every other day, using lukewarm water, lightly mist the paper towel through the tiny airholes in the plastic cover.

Adults and juveniles of the large form are impressive, alert, and inquisitive. Once settled in, they will take insect prey directly from your fingers, if desired. Also, include a slice of diced papaya for them at the base of the vivarium. Mist the lizards and the enclosure once daily. Include large branches, as well as a plant or two, to create areas for climbing and basking.

These lizards can be 'guided' with a hand placed near them to move onto the other hand or to a temporary container. Never attempt to grab or firmly hold this lizard as large sections of skin will come off in your hand, leaving large areas of pink flesh exposed on the lizard. Virtually every gecko specialist who has kept this species rates it very highly.

The Seychelles giant skin-sloughing day gecko *(Ailuronyx seychellensis)*, a magnificent ten inch long (25 cm) nocturnal "day gecko-like" lizard which shows specialized guarding behavior of its eggs. Photo by John Tashjian at the Chaffee Zoological Gardens of Fresno.

List of Species

P. a. abbotti -- Nosy Be, n. Madagascar, Aldabra Atoll (Seychelles)

P. abbotti sumptio -- Assumption Island (Seychelles)

P. andamanensis -- Andaman Islands in the Bay of Bengal (India)

P. a. astriata -- Mahé and s. granitic Seychelles

P. astriata semicarinata -- Praslin and n. granitic Seychelles

P. barbouri -- Central Madagascar

P. beufotakensis -- Nw. Madagascar

P. bimaculata -- E. Madagascar and islet of Ste. Marie

P. b. borbonica -- Reunion (overseas France)

P. borbonica agalegae -- Agalega Island (Mauritius)

P. breviceps -- Se. Madagascar

P. cepediana -- Mauritius

P. comorensis -- Grande Comoro (Comoro Islands)

P. dubia -- Nw. Madagascar, Comoros, Tanzania

P. edwardnewtonii EXTINCT -- Rodrigues (Mauritius)

P. flavigularis -- E. Madagascar

P. gigas EXTINCT -- Rodrigues (Mauritius)

P. guentheri -- Round Island (Mauritius)

P. g. guimbeaui -- Mauritius

P. guimbeaui rosagularis -- Mauritius

P. guttata -- E. Madagascar

P. klemmeri -- Nw. Madagascar

P. l. laticauda -- N. Madagascar, Comoros, Farquhar (Seychelles)

P. laticauda angularis -- Nw. Madagascar

P. leiogaster -- Sw. Madagascar

P. lineata lineata -- Central Madagascar

P. lineata bombetokensis -- W. Madagascar

P. lineata chloroscelis -- E. Madagascar

P. lineata dorsivittata -- N. Madagascar

P. lineata punctulata -- N. Madagascar

P. m. madagascariensis -- E. Madagascar

P. madagascariensis boehme -- E. Madagascar

P. madagascariensis grandis -- N. Madagascar

P. madagascariensis kochi -- W. Madagascar

P. minuthi -- Madagascar (Exact location unknown by author)

P. modesta -- S. Madagascar

P. mutabilis -- W. Madagascar

P. nigristriata -- Comoros

P. o. ornata -- Mauritius

P. ornata inexpectata -- Reunion (overseas France)

P. parkeri -- Pemba Island, Tanzania

P. p. pusilla -- E. Madagascar

P. pusilla hallmanni -- E. Madagascar

P. q. quadriocellata -- E. Madagascar

P. quadriocellata bimaculata -- E. Madagascar

P. quadriocellata leiura -- Se. Madagascar

P. quadriocellata parva -- E. Madagascar

P. robertmertensi -- Comoros

P. seippi -- Nosy Be, n. Madagascar

P. serraticauda -- E. Madagascar

P. standingi -- Sw. Madagascar

P. s. sundbergi -- Praslin, Curieuse (Seychelles)

P. sundbergi ladiguensis -- La Digue, Marianne (Seychelles)

P. sundbergi longisulae -- Mahé, s. granitic Seychelles

P. trilineata -- Origin not known

P. v-nigra v-nigra -- Moheli Island (Comoros)

P. v-nigra anjouanensis -- Anjouan Island (Comoros)

P. v-nigra comoraegrandensis -- Grande Comoro (Comoros)

P. v-nigra pasteuri -- Comoros

GLOSSARY

Acclimation. The adjustment of an animal to its surroundings when in captivity.

Aestivation. A prolonged inactivity during the hottest periods of the year.

Anterior. Toward the head or forward end of an animal.

Antibiotic. A general term for a drug that will kill or control pathogenic microorganisms.

Arboreal. Dwelling in shrubs or trees.

Bask. To place the body or a section of the body in a position directly exposed to the sun.

Calcareous. Consisting of or containing calcium carbonate.

Cloaca. The common chamber in reptiles and amphibians into which the digestive, urinary, and reproductive canals discharge their contents, and which opens to the exterior through the anus.

Clutch. The eggs produced by a single female animal as a result of one breeding effort.

Courtship. Ritualized behavioral interractions between males and females that preceed and accompany mating. This behavior is highly developed in day geckos and includes a series of distinctive visual signals or cues. These signals, if successful, include the approach, close contact, ritualized movements, and actual mating.

Crepuscular. Active at twilight periods (dusk or dawn).

Desiccation. The process of drying out. In day geckos, this may apply to both eggs and the actual lizard if air moisture levels become too low.

Display. A specific pattern of behavior involved in communication between animals. It includes any of the senses such as vision, hearing, touch, and smell.

Diurnal. Active during the daytime.

Dorsal. Of or pertaining to the back or upper surface of the body.

Dorsolateral. Of or pertaining to the upper sides of the body.

Ectoparasite. A parasite that inhabits the outer surface of an organism, e.g., a mite or tick.

Ectothermic. Regulating the body temperature by means of outside sources of heat, such as the sun (= cold-blooded).

Egg-laying. A female day gecko typically lays her eggs beneath bark, inside a tree hollow or, depending on the species, beneath a log or rock, or other suitable place where the humidity is relatively high and the temperature more constant than in an unprotected location.

Endemic. Confined to a certain area, region, group of islands, or continent and found nowhere else.

Endothermic. Regulating the body temperature by means of an internal regulating mechanism so as to produce a more-or-less conxstant body temperature (= warm-blooded).

Family. A taxonomic category ranking below order and above genus.

Femoral pores. Small openings on the underside of the thighs in some species of lizard, which secrete a waxlike substance.

Fertilization. In day geckos, fertilization of one or more eggs occurs inside the female's oviducts, and the embryo achieves some development prior to laying.

Fossorial. Adapted for and leading primarily a burrowing existence.

Gecko. Members of this large family of lizards are notable for their abilities to vocalize and, in many cases, to climb, even on slick vertical surfaces. Widely distributed in both the Old and New World and on oceanic islands, they are especially diverse in the tropics. Climbing geckos, such as day geckos, have individual rows of scales on the undersides of their toes referred to as setae.

Genus (pl. genera). A taxonomic category above species and below family. In a scientific name, the genus comes before the species name; the first letter is always capitalized.

Gestation. The period of development or carrying of embryos (within the body) by the female of a species.

Granules. Tiny, flat scales.

Gravid. A female bearing eggs or young, ordinarily in the oviducts (pregnant).

Gregarious. Tending to congregate into groups.

Gular fold. Fold of skin across the rear of the throat, well-developed in certain lizards.

Hemipenis (pl. hemipenes). One of the grooved, paired copulatory organs (double penis), found in lizards and snakes. A male lizard's hemipenes are elongated, rounded pouches which are turned outward during copulation. One is used at each mating. When not in use, they are sheathed in the lateral areas of the ventral portion of the tail.

Herpetology. The study of reptiles and amphibians.

Herptile. Any individual reptile or amphibian.

Indigenous. Occurring or living naturally in a particular region or place, but not restricted in distribution to that area.

Interspecific. Occurring between members of different species.

Intraspecific. Occurring within or between members of the same species.

Jacobson's organ. One of the primary sensory organs in snakes and many lizards. This organ is located in the roof of the mouth and is used to perceive odors and chemical substances.

Juvenile. A young, not yet sexually mature individual, sometimes displaying proportions and coloration which differ from that of the adult.

Labial. Of or pertaining to the lips.

Lateral. Of or pertaining to the side.

Mascarene Islands. This term refers collectively to the three western Indian Ocean volcanic islands of Mauritius, Reunion, and Rodrigues and their offshore islets.

Melanistic. Having an abundance of black, resulting in an all-black or unusually dark animal; the opposite of albinism.

Mid-dorsal. Of or pertaining to the center of the upper surface of the body.

Mid-ventral. Of or pertaining to the center of the undersurface of the body or abdomen.

Montane. Of or pertaining to mountains, or living at higher elevations.

Neonate. A young animal that has just emerged from its egg, or which has just been born.

Nocturnal. Active primarily at night.

Nominate. Referring to the first or originally described form or type of a given species.

Omnivorous. Feeding on both animal and plant material.

Oviparous. Reproducing by means of eggs that hatch outside the body of the female.

Ovoviviparous. Reproducing by means of eggs that have a shell, but which hatch inside the female before or just before laying so as to produce living young.

Pantropic. Occurring or distributed throughout the tropical regions of the world.

Pathogenic. Disease-causing. Examples include bacteria and many viruses.

Pectoral. Of or pertaining to the chest.

Pharynx. The portion of the alimentary canal between the cavity of the mouth and the esophagus.

Preanal scales. Scales located on the ventral surface anterior to the anus. In males of some geckos and certain other lizards, these scales may have enlarged pores that secrete a waxlike substance.

Predation. Obtaining food through consumption of prey animals which may be either vertebrates or invertebrates.

Prehensile. Adapted for grasping or seizing, especially by wrapping around, as the tails of certain lizards and snakes.

Resource partitioning. Referring to the utilization of separate or different portions of the same habitat so as not to compete directly for existing resources. This term may be applied to separate species or to different age groups within a species.

Reticulations. A network-type pattern of markings.

Riparian. Living at the edge of or in close proximity to a river, stream, or similar body of fresh water.

Scale. A thin, flattened platelike structure forming the major part of the surface covering of reptiles and certain other vertebrates.

Scute. Any enlarged scale of a reptile which may also be referred to as a "plate" or "shield."

Sexual dichromatism. Sexually dimorphic in color. Typically, the adult males are the most colorful.

Sexual dimorphism. A difference between males and females of the same species in color, form, or structure.

Snout-vent length. The direct or straight line length of a reptile, amphibian, or other animal as measured from the anterior tip of the snout to the posterior tip of the vent.

Species. A group of animals that naturally interbreeds to produce fertile offspring. The fundamental unit of classification.

Subadult. A young individual that is older and/or larger than a juvenile, but which has not yet achieved full adult size. Subadults may be capable of breeding although, if social, have not as yet obtained a high rank within the group.

Subcaudal. Beneath or on the ventral surface of the tail.

Subspecies. When a population of animals is distributed over a geographic area with diverse environmental conditions, the members of the species in one section of the range may differ slightly in form or color from those in another section. Each subdivision is known as a race or subspecies.

Substrate. The material which is used on the bottom of a vivarium, such as soil, newspaper, or bark.

Sympatric. A term applied to two or more populations of animals that occupy the same or overlapping geographical areas.

Taxon (pl. taxa). A specific taxonomic group or entity such as a species or subspecies.

Terrestrial. Living primarily on land or on flat surfaces.

Territorial. Defending an area so as to exclude other members of the same species.

Threat display. A social behavior to indicate territorial ownership or agressive intent. With day geckos, this behavior is usually directed towards members of the same species in the form of specific color changes, tail-waving, and head movements.

Total length. The greatest straightline length of a reptile, amphibian or other animal as measured from the anterior tip of the snout to the posterior tip of the tail.

Vent. The ventral opening of the cloaca which serves as the terminus of waste discharge and the reproductive canal; in snakes and lizards the vent is considered the division between the body and tail.

Ventral. Of or pertaining to the underside of the body.

Vertical pupil. A vertically elliptical pupil of the eye that is especially useful to animals active at night.

Vestigial. Referring to a small and degenerate or imperfectly developed bodily part or organ that remains from one more fully developed in an earlier stage of the individual, in a past form, or closely related forms.

Visual signals. Many lizards, including day geckos, use these distinctive behaviors in courtship. In day geckos, the male may begin by moving his head and upper body in a series of lateral movements. If receptive, the female will respond with her own visual cues. Visual signals are extremely important in day gecko courtship and usually involve movements of the head, body, and tail.

Vivarium. An enclosure for keeping or raising and observing animals indoors.

Vocalization. Day geckos have well-formed vocal chords and a diverse vocal repertoire. Day geckos of both sexes are able to make a series of auditory sounds or vocalizations. Often these noises, a series of modulated chirps and clicks, vary according to the social situation, such as territorial defense, courtship, and mating. Specific noises may also be used to voice alarm.

SOURCE MATERIALS

Bloxam, Q. 1980. Maintenance and breeding of *Phelsuma guentheri* (Boulenger, 1885). In The British Herpetological Society: The Care and Breeding of Captive Reptiles, 51-62.

Bloxam, Q. and M. Vokins. 1978. Breeding and maintenance of *Phelsuma guentheri* (Boulenger, 1885) at the Jersey Zoological Park. Dodo, J. Jersey Wildlife Preservation Trust 15: 82-91.

Bohme, W. & Meier, H. 1981. Eine neue form der *madagascariensis* - gruppe der gattung *Phelsuma* von den Seychellen. (Reptilia: Sauria: Gekkonidae). Salamandra 17: 12-19.

Borner, A.R. 1972. Revision der geckonidengattung *Phelsuma* (Gray, 1825). Cologne: A.R. Borner. Private publication.

Borner, A.R. & W. Minuth. 1982. Advance diagnoses of new taxa of the *Phelsuma madagascariensis* group. Misc. Artic. Saurol. No. 11: 1-19. Cologne.

Cheke, A.S. 1982. *Phelsuma* (Gray, 1825) in the Seychelles and neighbouring islands: a reappraisal of their taxonomy and description of two new forms. Senchenbergiana Biologica 62: 181-198.

Digney, T. & T. Tytle. 1983. Captive maintenance and propagation of the lizard genus *Phelsuma*. In Proceedings of the Sixth Annual Reptile Symposium on Captive Propagation and Husbandry 141-156. D. Marcellini (ed.). Thurmont, Maryland: Zoological Consortium.

Gardner, A.S. 1984. The evolutionary ecology and population systematics of day geckos *(Phelsuma)* in the Seychelles. Unpublished Ph.D. Dissertation, University of Aberdeen, Scotland.

Gardner, A.S. 1987. The systematics of the *Phelsuma madagascariensis* group of day geckos (Reptilia: Gekkonidae) in the Seychelles. Zoological Journal of the Linnean Society 91: 93-105.

Henkel, F.-W. & W. Schmidt. 1991. Geckos: Biologie, Haltung und Zucht. Ulmer GmbH & Co. Stuttgart, Germany.

McKeown, S. 1983. Wild status and captive management of Indian Ocean *Phelsuma* with special reference to the Mauritius Lowland Forest Day Gecko *(Phelsuma g. guimbeaui)*. In Proceedings of the Sixth Annual Reptile Symposium on Captive Propagation and Husbandry, 157-170. D. Marcellini (ed.). Thurmont, Maryland: Zoological Consortium.

McKeown, S. 1984. Management and propagation of the lizard genus *Phelsuma*. Acta Zoologica et Path. Antverpiensia 78 (1): 149-161. V/ Bels & A.P. Van Den Sande, P. (eds). Antwerp.

McKeown, S. 1988. Mauritius Lowland Forest Day Geckos hatched at the Fresno Zoo. In AAZPA Communique Spring: 22.

McKeown, S. 1989. Breeding and Maintenance of the Mauritius Lowland Forest Day Gecko *(Phelsuma g. guimbeaui)* at the Fresno Zoo. International Zoo Yearbook 28. P.J.S. Olney & P. Ellis (eds.). Zool. Soc. of London.

McKeown, S. 1991. Day Geckos, genus *Phelsuma* : an overview of their wild status and captive management. In Proceedings of the 2nd Herpetological Assoc. of Africa Conference. W.R. Branch, G.V. Haagner & R.C. Boycott (eds.) Bloemfontein, South Africa.

Meier, H. 1981. *Phelsuma robertmertensi* ein neuer Taggecko. Herpetofauna 11: 6-8.

Meier, H. 1982. Ergebnisse zur Taxonomie und Okologie einiger Arten und Unterarten der Gattung *Phelsuma* auf Madagaskar, gesammelt in den Jahren 1972 bis 1981, mit Beschreibung einer neuen Form. Salamandra 18 (3/4): 168-190.

Meier, H. 1986. Der Formenkreis von *Phelsuma v-nigra* (Boettger, 1913) (Sauria: Geckkonidae) auf den Komoren: Beschreibung von zwei neuen Unterarten. Salamandra 22 (1): 11-20.

Meier, H. 1989a. Zur Faunistik madagassischer Taggeckos der Gattung *Phelsuma* ostlich von Fianarantsoa, bei Tamatave und auf der Insel Ste. Marie. Salamandra 25 (3/4): 224-229.

Meier, H. 1989b. Eine neue Form aus der *lineata*-Gruppe der Gattung *Phelsuma* auf Madagaskar. Salamandra 25 (3/4): 230-236.

Meier, H. & W. Boehme. 1990. Notes on habitat selection and colouration in life of *Phelsuma borbonica agalegae* (Cheke,1975) (Reptilia: Gekkonidae). British Herpetological Society Bulletin 33: 4-8.

Meier, H. & W. Bohme. 1991. Zue Arealkunde von *Phelsuma madagascariensis* (Gray, 1831) andhand der Museumssammlungen A. Koenig und Senckenberg, mit Bemerkungen zur Variabilitat von *P. m. kochi* Mertens, 1954. Salamandra 27 (3): 143-151.

Mertens, R. 1954. Eine neue Rasse von *Phelsuma madagascariensis*. Senck. Biol. 35 (1/2): 13-16.

Mertens, R. 1962. Die arten und unterarten der geckonengattung *Phelsuma*. Senck. Biol. 43: 87-127.

Mertens, R. 1963. Zwei neue Arten der Geckonengattung *Phelsuma*. Senck. Biol. 44 (5): 349-356.

Mertens, R. 1964. Funf neue Rassen der Geckonengattung *Phelsuma*. Senck. Biol. 45 (2): 99-112.

Mertens, R. 1966. Die nictmadagassischen Arten und Unterarten der Geckonengattung *Phelsuma*. Senck. Biol. 47 (2): 85-110.

Mertens, R. 1970. Neues uber einige Taxa der Geckonengattung *Phelsuma*. Senck. Biol. 51 (1/2): 1-13.

Mertens, R. 1973. Eine neue Unterart des Taggeckos *Phelsuma lineata*. Senck. Biol. 54 (4/6): 299-301.

Miller, M. J. 1982. Phelsumas: A case of monotypic care of a polytypic genus. In Proceedings 5th Annual Reptile Symposium on Captive Propagation and Husbandry: 103-118. Marcellini, D. (Ed.). Thurmont, Maryland: Zoological Consortium.

Osadnik, G. 1984. An investigation of egg laying in *Phelsuma*. Amphibia-Reptilia 5: 125-134.

Ratnam, Jayashree. Distribution and behavioural ecology of the Andaman day gecko *(Phelsuma andamanensis)*. Unpublished master's thesis, Pondicherry University, India.

Rendahl, H. 1939. Zur herpetologie der Seychellen. I. Reptilien. Zoologische Fahrbucher Abteilungen Systematik, Okologie und Geographie der Tiere 72: 157-328.

Seufer, Hermann. 1991. Keeping and Breeding Geckos. T.F.H. Publications, Inc., Neptune, N.J. 128-150.

Seipp, R. 1991. Eine neue Art der Gattung *Phelsuma* Gray 1825 von Madagaskar. Senck. biol. 71 (3/4): 11-14.

Tytle, T. 1986. Calcium metabolism in the lizard genus *Phelsuma:* a preliminary report. In Proceedings 9th International Herpetological Symposium on Captive Propagation and Husbandry : 175-183. S. McKeown, F. Caporaso, & K.H. Peterson (eds). Thurmont, Maryland: Zoological Consortium.

Tytle, T. 1989. Day Geckos: *Phelsuma*; The captive maintenance and propagation of day geckos. The Vivarium 2(5): 15,18,19,29. S. McKeown (ed.).

Viets, B. 1990. An investigation into the possible adaptive significance of temperature-dependent sex determination in reptiles: the effects of temperature on sex determination development and growth in the lizard *Anolis carolinensis*. Research Proposal. Department of Biology, Indiana University. 1-68.

Vinson, J.M. 1975. Notes on the reptiles of Round Island. Mauritius Institute Bulletin 8 (1): 49-67.

Vinson, J.M. 1976. The saurian fauna of the Mascarene Islands. The distribution of *Phelsuma* species in Mauritius. Mauritius Institute Bulletin 8 (2): 177-195.

Vinson, J. & J.M. Vinson. 1969. The saurian fauna of the Mascarene Islands. Mauritius Institute Bulletin 6 (4): 203-320.